LIVING WELL
WITH CELIAC DISEASE
Second Edition

Abundance Beyond Wheat and Gluten

Claudine Crangle

Foreword by Cynthia Rudert, M.D.,
Medical Advisor for the Celiac Disease Foundation
and the Gluten Intolerance Group of America

⊘ YOUR HEALTH PRESS

LIVING WELL

WITH CELIAC DISEASE
Second Edition

Abundance Beyond Wheat and Gluten

First published in Canada in 2002 by
Your Health Press™, a division of Sarahealth Inc.
in association with Trafford Publishing.

National Library of Canada Cataloguing in Publication

Crangle, Claudine
    Living well with celiac disease : abundance beyond wheat and
gluten / Claudine Crangle.

Includes bibliographical references.
ISBN 1-55369-404-X

    1. Gluten-free diet. 2. Celiac disease—Diet therapy. 3. Celiac
disease—Popular works. I. Title.

RM237.86.C73 2002   641.5'63   C2002-901657-6

Your Health Press™
A division of Sarahealth Inc.
Printed in Canada

IMPORTANT NOTICE:

The purpose of this book is to educate. It is sold with the understanding that the author shall have neither liability nor responsibility for any injury caused or alleged to be caused directly or indirectly by the information contained in this book. While every effort has been made to ensure its accuracy, the book's contents should not be construed as medical advice. Each person's health needs are unique. To obtain recommendations appropriate to your particular situation, please consult a qualified health care provider. Any herbal information in this book is provided for educational purposes only and is not meant to be used without consulting a qualified health practitioner who is trained in herbal medicine. Please note that the recipes in this book have not been test-kitchened.

This book was published *on-demand* in cooperation with Trafford Publishing.
On-demand publishing is a unique process and service of making a book available for retail sale to the public taking advantage of on-demand manufacturing and Internet marketing.
On-demand publishing includes promotions, retail sales, manufacturing, order fulfilment, accounting and collecting royalties on behalf of the author.

Suite 6E, 2333 Government St., Victoria, B.C. V8T 4P4, CANADA

Phone	250-383-6864	Toll-free	1-888-232-4444 (Canada & US)
Fax	250-383-6804	E-mail	orders@trafford.com
Web site	www.trafford.com	TRAFFORD PUBLISHING IS A DIVISION OF TRAFFORD HOLDINGS LTD.	
Trafford Catalogue #02-0217		www.trafford.com/02-0217	

15   14   13   12   11   10

YOUR HEALTH PRESS

A line of health books dedicated to orphan conditions and rare, contro-versial, or stigmatizing health topics you won't find in regular book-stores. Your Health Press titles are available only at online bookstores such as *amazon.com*. Visit *www.yourhealthpress.com* for more details.

Stopping Cancer at the Source by M. Sara Rosenthal, Ph.D. (2001)

Women and Unwanted Hair by M. Sara Rosenthal, Ph.D. (2001)

Living Well with an Ostomy by Elizabeth Rayson (2003)

The Thyroid Cancer Book, Second Edition by M. Sara Rosenthal, Ph.D. (2003)

Thyroid Eye Disease: Understanding Graves' Ophthalmopathy by Elaine A. Moore (2003)

Healing Injuries the Natural Way: How to Mend Bones, Muscles, Tendons & More by Michelle Cook (2004)

Menopause Before 40: Coping with Premature Ovarian Failure by Karin Banerd (2004)

The Low Iodine Cookbook: Easy and Delicious Recipes for the Low Iodine Diet by Norene Gilletz (2005)

ACKNOWLEDGEMENTS

I wish to thank Dr. Cynthia Rudert, M.D., F.A.C.P., Dr. Ralph Warren, M.D., F.R.C.P.C, D.T.M.&H., and Shelley Case, R.D., for their support and guidance with the medical information in this book. I would also like to show my appreciation to Bev Ruffo of the Canadian Celiac Association and Claire Anderson of the Ontario Liquor Control Board.

Thanks to the volunteer members of the Celiac Associations world-wide, who sent me endless emails, updates, and well-wishes for the book. There's also a very long list of helpful restaurant owners, chefs, and merchants to whom I am indebted.

This work became a book thanks to the efforts of Larissa Kostoff, Laura Tulchinsky and Sara Rosenthal at Your Health Press. You just never know who you'll meet at a party.

And finally, without sounding like an academy award speech, I wish to extend my gratitude to my mother Celia, a true pioneer, Sarah Baillie for showing me the "path," and Danielle Bobker, without whom I would never have got past page one. Danielle, I dedicate this book to you.

CONTENTS

FOREWORD

We are certainly living in a time of increased research and an explosion of information on Celiac Disease. It is now known that Celiac Disease is the most common inherited autoimmune illness of humankind and is thought to affect one in every 266 people worldwide. Thanks to research performed by Dr. Fasano and his colleagues, it is now known that one in every 133 Americans has this commonly missed autoimmune illness. It was not that long ago when reports in medical literature were few and far between regarding Celiac Disease; however, now it is unusual for me to pick up a medical journal or a medical review article without some mention of this common disorder.

One certainly can live well with Celiac Disease and, in fact, many of the popular diets followed by Americans today are actually severely gluten-restricted or gluten-free. So there are many individuals, not only Celiacs, that are electing to follow a gluten-free diet for a healthy lifestyle.

I refer to Celiac Disease as a chameleon-like illness since it presents in so many different ways. In fact, in the hundreds of individuals I am following many are unique in their presentations. You can have Celiac Disease and be overweight, underweight, tall or short and even with or without gastrointestinal symptoms. In fact, the face of Celiac Disease is as diverse as our general population.

It is gratifying for me as a physician to be able to work with individuals on a common disorder that is treated only by diet and where almost everyone significantly improves.

If you take everyone with ulcerative colitis and all patients with Crohn's Disease and Cystic Fibrosis and double this number, this is how many individuals are estimated to have Celiac Disease. The vast majority are yet to be diagnosed.

I am certain you will enjoy Ms. Claudine Crangle's book as well as I have. I recommend it to all my patients.

Cynthia S. Rudert, M.D., F.A.C.P.
Medical Advisor, Celiac Disease Foundation
Medical Advisor, Gluten Intolerance Group of America
Private Practice – Gastroenterology, Atlanta, Georgia
Dr. Rudert has one of the largest practices in North America dedicated to Celiac Disease and treats patients from all over the world.

INTRODUCTION

Gone Are the Days of the Flour Child

My parents bragged about having the perfect baby—at least until I began gnawing on teething biscuits. Every parent anticipates the terrible twos, but things just got progressively worse. By the time I was three I needed an exorcism.

My mother tells me that I would sit jammed between her legs and the kitchen cupboards screaming for hours with my frail arms wrapped tightly around her ankles as she washed dishes and cooked supper. Today, Children's Aid or Social Services would investigate the parents of a child who made regular visits to emergency for broken limbs. Instead, doctors told my mother that the little girl with sunken eyes and a pot-belly that screamed of starvation was simply a neurotic child.

On my fourth birthday, my baby brother was bigger than I was. Ironically, I received a set of cake mixes for the Easy Bake Oven I hoped to someday own. It's not a rare occurrence for a child to behave poorly at her birthday party, but I understand that I was a sickly little psycho terror. Finally, after almost three years of insanity, my mother reached the end of her rope. She handed my shell to the doctor and told him to do something with me or they would have to lock her up.

I spent many weeks undergoing prodding and tests. I moved into two different hospitals over a couple of months, while doctors tried to figure out why my little body was dying of malnutrition. It was our family GP who finally came up with the suggestion that I be tested for celiac disease. After a biopsy and positive diagnosis, my mother was handed a diet to follow and I was released from the world of metal bed frames.

Within weeks, my emaciated body began to fill out, and a new child emerged. Aside from my tiny stature, I was starting to look like any other kid about to enter kindergarten.

My mom stayed home and spent many a day experimenting with the one cookbook available to her. Many of these experiments never met my lips, but instead went straight from the baking sheet to the bin. The ingredients we take for granted these days were not as widely available as they are now and allergies and intolerance of foods were not nearly as socially understood, nor were they catered to. In 1972, health food stores were musty little places where the hippies shopped. And no one else was asking for soy flour.

My friends will tell you that when I first moved out on my own, I'd consider a can of nuked green beans and a bag of potato chips dinner. Chocolate was always on hand, and the coffeepot was forever brewing. I was gluten free.

At 25, I moved to Italy and spent my first summer living with an East Indian and Italian couple. These were worldly people who introduced me to new flavor combinations in the simplest of foods. In the fall, I moved in with an old-school Italian man, and suddenly I was the person responsible to shop for and cook the meals if I was going to eat.

I had to learn fast. I picked up my Italian vocabulary in the kitchens of the neighbors and my friends' mothers. And it was in these kitchens that I acquired the pleasure of cooking and sharing food with others. I loved food, and the mothers loved my appetite. *"Mangia bene!"*

Even with all of that wonderful healthy food around I was unable to satiate my appetite for the fine gluten-free cookies, cakes, and chocolate bars available in Europe. My last week in Italy was spent in a Roman hospital where a case of suspected appendicitis turned out to be an ovarian cyst. I returned home to Canada overweight and lethargic. My friend Sarah, who was studying naturopathic medicine, suggested that I make a trip to the clinic.

I believed I was very conscious of what went into my mouth. It wasn't until I was asked to do a diet diary that I realized I was eating a lot of flour—albeit gluten-free—and hence my diet was full of carbs and refined sugars. Living on a gluten-free diet doesn't necessarily mean living healthy. It was time to take a new look at what I'd been putting into my body. It was also time to take a hard look at the excuses I'd been making about all the junk I'd been eating because I was "so limited."

What a difference a diet makes. Again, it only took a few weeks to feel the benefits of a few simple changes. With the help of my naturopath, in three months I was in better shape than I'd ever been before. I'd finally signed a peace agreement with food, and the story of what happened in my subsequent explorations will follow in the chapters ahead.

1

THE FACTS

What's the Damage?

So Life's Not Going to be a Cakewalk:
Understanding Celiac Disease

The fact that you will never stuff another cheese Danish in your mouth without suffering some nasty consequence is actually a gift. Perhaps I have my head half shaved and am sporting a toga as I mutter my mantra to the god of rice cakes, but I *have* chosen my reality. I'm not crazy. I simply prefer to think it's empowering to reclaim your health by ignoring English muffins.

When you first discover that you're unable to enjoy some of the foods you love, it's natural to be torn in two. There's the sense of relief that comes from finally knowing what to avoid so that you don't feel ill anymore. But there's also a sense of loss.

Peers shuffle uncomfortably in their seats as you torture the waiter with a barrage of questions over a bowl of minestrone soup. You're afraid to let little Ben go to his friend's birthday party unless you can be there to watch him like a hawk. A weekend at your cousin Linda's cottage means six extra bags of food to pack. You can just imagine a sightseeing trip to Paris.

Breathe. This book is going to show you the ropes. Unlike other books on the topic of gluten-free diets, this isn't a cookbook; it's a cope book. I can assure you, however, that when armed with the right tools, you'll do a lot better than just cope.

A couple of practical notes: I often use the term "free" in this book to describe anything that is gluten-free. This naturally covers the wheat-free issue as well. Emphasizing the positive rather than the part we *can't* have is the first step towards a healthier attitude. And who doesn't jump at the chance to try things when they're free?

Those with wheat intolerance have a few more options than do those with gluten intolerance, but both will benefit from the ideas in this book. Rather than considering dos and don'ts for each, I've focused on the gluten-free diet, thus eliminating some potential confusion.

Finally, I should note that I've chosen not to refer to any brand names when it comes to "free" choices. This was a conscious decision, as availability of products from coast to coast differs. More importantly, ingredients of products change. Manufacturers also produce their products in more than one facility, and not always in the same way.

What I offer in this book is 30 years of experience with celiac disease and gluten intolerance. This is not a medical reference. I'll leave the science to the professionals. This is a practical guide to day-to-day living. I've learned the difference between staying alive by following the rules and really taking charge of my health and the *quality* of my life as it pertains to food. The aim of this book is to help you to put your food intolerance in perspective, and more importantly, to get you feeling good, even *great*, about life on a "free" diet!

Down the Tubes: How the GI Tract Works

Celiac disease sure sounds scary, maybe even contagious, but it's only ugly if left undiagnosed. And even a diagnosis can leave you in the dark. It's important to understand that celiac disease involves sections of the GI tract. My aim here is to simplify and clarify the condition so that you'll be able to explain it yourself. (You'll find it the topic of a lot of dinner conversations.)

When I was five, I told people I had "silly-act" disease. I was confused. Celia is my mother's name. Celiac disease (spelled coeliac in Britain and much of Europe) is a condition also referred to as celiac sprue, celiac syndrome, nontropical sprue, gluten-sensitive enteropathy, and gluten-enteropathy. What a mouthful.

People with celiac disease need to avoid ingesting gluten. Gluten is a mixture of proteins found in grains, including some grains that are tolerated by celiacs (like corn, for example). What we *can't* tolerate is gliadin, a specific protein found in the gluten of wheat, barley, triticale, rye, and oats. We call it *gluten intolerance*, but in fact it's the *gliadin* to which the body responds negatively.

The reason a celiac patient can't tolerate this gluten is still not fully understood. We know that celiac disease is an autoimmune disorder wherein the body produces antibodies in response to gluten. These antibodies not only attack the gluten protein, but also wage an attack on the cells of the body that have started to absorb the gluten. This sabotage takes place in the small intestine, which is a winding hose that is about 15 feet long. The small intestine is composed of the duodenum, the jejunum, and the ileum. Food makes its way from the stomach into the small intestine through the duodenum. From here, it travels through the winding intestine or jejunum and exits through the ileum, which is the section that attaches the small intestine to the large intestine—also known as the colon.

The major functions of the intestinal tract are digestion and absorption. The inside of the small intestine is lined with little fingers called villi. Each of these little fingers is further coated with more little fingers called microvilli. The purpose of all of these fingers upon fingers is to increase the surface space of the small intestine, and also to provide a sort of traction that allows nutrients to be drawn from food.

Imagine a celiac eats a piece of bread. Once the bread enters the small intestine, the body's immune system begins to send antibodies after the gluten toxin. As the villi begin to absorb the gluten, the antibodies assault the villi themselves. The result is that the villi become worn down and flattened. And as the villi are destroyed, so is the body's ability to absorb nutrients. The result is malnutrition, which in turn brings on a barrage of other ailments.

So how do you know you have celiac disease? Well, chances are if you're reading this book, you've already been diagnosed. It can take years for most people to finally be diagnosed with CD. And because of the broad spectrum of possible symptoms, it can be very difficult to diagnose properly.

Belly Aching: The Symptoms of Celiac Disease

Symptoms can range in their severity for a couple of reasons. First, there is the extent of intestinal tract that's been affected. Damage starts at the duodenum and works its way down. As long as there is a sufficient length of intestine left undamaged, the body may continue to absorb nutrients to the extent that problems are not evident. This is often referred to as "silent" celiac. Overt celiac symptoms occur when the damage is so widespread that the body is unable to absorb nutrients. The severity of symptoms is also affected by the length of time the body has been inadequately nourished.

Celiac disease has generally been associated with symptoms in and around the gut; but in some cases the only symptoms that may be present are fatigue or anemia. Anemia is a result of iron and/or folic acid deficiency. These minerals are absorbed in the duodenum, and since the duodenum is the first part of the intestinal tract, it's also the first part to suffer the consequences of gluten. Other symptoms you'll see listed below occur as a result of malnutrition.

In adult patients, symptoms can include one or a combination of problems in the following areas:

The gut
- Weight loss
- Abdominal bloating and gas
- Recurrent abdominal pain
- Recurrent diarrhea
- Nausea and vomiting
- Lactose intolerance

The mouth
- Mouth ulcers
- Dental enamel defects

The bones
- Bone or joint pain
- Osteoporosis
- Short stature

The hormones

- Amenorrhea (lack of menstrual periods)
- Infertility in women
- Impotence in men

The emotions

- Depression and lethargy
- Irritability
- Inability to concentrate

Other symptoms

- Chronic fatigue and weakness
- Anemia (deficiency of iron or folic acid or both)

Dermatitis herpetiformis (DH) is another condition that is closely related to celiac disease. DH appears as a very itchy rash, with eruptions that are bumpy and blister-like. DH occurs as a result of a gluten intolerance, and can be controlled with a gluten-free diet. In addition, a doctor may prescribe a topical medication.

While small children are still frequently misdiagnosed, they exhibit symptoms that are generally more typical than they are in adults. Symptoms first appear once a child is introduced to solid food—specifically gluten-containing baby cereals—and will gain momentum as the child's diet of gluten increases. Typical symptoms include:

Physiological

- Weight loss
- Failure to gain weight or thrive
- Wasted or flattened buttocks
- Swollen abdomen
- Pale and undernourished appearance (even though eating a "healthy" diet)
- Steatorrhea (large, pale stools)
- Vomiting and/or diarrhea
- Bloating and gas
- Short stature compared to other children their age

Behavioral

- Listlessness
- Irritability
- Stubbornness or disruptive behavior
- Hyperactivity
- Inability to concentrate
- Inconsolable crying fits

Older children often suffer from delayed puberty in untreated celiac disease.

It was once believed that celiac was a disease of childhood, and that the child would grow out of it. Today we know that this simply isn't true. For reasons unknown, symptoms can go into a form of remission during puberty. This doesn't mean, however, that the damage occurring as a result of the ingested gluten stops. Usually, the physiological symptoms reappear in early adulthood, but they may not show up again until later in life. Unfortunately, without the symptoms, many assume that they've "grown out of it," and it's not until some unfortunate side effects of gluten toxicity rear themselves that a problem is again acknowledged.

The results of long-term damage can include many of the ailments listed above, including infertility in women, miscarriage, and osteoporosis, all three of which are due to a lack of nutrients, and worse, lymphoma (specifically small bowel cancer). Reason enough to carry on with a gluten-free diet, even if symptoms temporarily subside. These symptoms—bad as they can be—are in fact protecting you from further harm by telling you that something is wrong!

The Inside Scoop: Diagnostic Tests for Celiac Disease

Celiac disease is often misdiagnosed as a number of other ailments, including Crohn's disease, irritable bowel syndrome, or chronic fatigue syndrome. The only way to absolutely confirm that a patient is indeed suffering from celiac disease is by way of a small bowel biopsy.

This is an outpatient procedure that may or may not have you sedated. It involves the use of a long, flexible tube called an endoscope, which is inserted into your mouth and then moved just past the stomach into the small intestine. From here, via a tiny camera in the tube, the doctor doing the procedure can see the intestinal lining, and can also remove small pieces of tissue for further examination in the lab. It is most important that the patient does *not* start on a gluten-free diet prior to the biopsy, as this could dramatically affect the results of the tests.

Some hospitals and clinics are adopting the new "capsule" endoscopy as an option to the traditional tube system. The patient simply swallows a pill-sized capsule that is equipped with a digital camera. This tiny instrument sends photos to a recording device that is attached to the patient's waist while he wanders around or watches television. The disposable capsule passes through the digestive system like food in about eight hours. Very civilized. Sign me up.

Blood tests are also available, and are especially important for screening purposes. The blood tests are called the IgA endomysium (EmA) and the IgA tissue transglutaminase (tTG) antibody tests. As celiac disease is a genetic disorder, these tests can help to determine whether or not family members are carrying the celiac gene, and thus should have a biopsy.

As a result of these tests, there has been much discussion regarding the prevalence of celiac disease. There are certain areas in the world, such as Denmark and Sweden, where blood screening has confirmed celiac disease to be as prevalent as 1 in 300. Much of Europe, including Ireland and Italy, considers these figures to be an accurate ratio, and as a result their governments have systems in place to screen for and subsidize those with celiac. There are no "hard" numbers, however, for North America, where estimates range anywhere from 1 in 250 to 1 in 1,000.

Given that we're dealing with a genetic disorder, on a continent where so much of the population is of European ancestry, it's surprising that our medical communities have been slow to embrace the findings of the European researchers. That said, there are presently some very important studies taking place in the U.S. that aim to trace the prevalence of celiac disease. It's anticipated that this research will reveal some reliable numbers for us to work with within the next couple of years.

As a group that is constantly misdiagnosed, celiacs cost the health care system a small fortune! Yet as long as our governments view celiac as a rare disease, and are unable to see the cost that it imposes on their health care budgets, there will be little funding made available for screening and research.

On the Topic of Research...

Some research groups are focusing on ways to destroy the toxicity of gluten proteins with an enzyme-type therapy (not unlike the lactose enzyme that those with lactose intolerance can take before ingesting milk). There are complications, however, and there are issues surrounding timing and functionality when taking a pill with food. Should this kind of therapy become available, it would likely supplement a gluten-free diet.

Other researchers are looking at ways to block the release of a protein called zonulin, which regulates how the intestines absorb food. They have learned that gliadin (gluten) induces the production of zonulin in celiac patients. If too much zonulin is produced, the intestinal wall becomes very permeable, allowing toxins to have easier access to the immune system, triggering an autoimmune response. Human clinical trials for a drug to block zonulin production may soon be underway.

While it is a comfort to know that there is ongoing research on our behalf, it appears that we will not likely see pharmaceuticals available in the immediate future. Until we know the long-term results of adopting any potential therapy...hold the bun.

For now, the most important thing to learn is how not to ingest any of this detrimental gluten. The next chapter will help clarify what exactly the doctors want you to avoid. It will also help arm you with the tools you'll need to detect some of the not-so-obvious places gluten is lurking.

2
THE FOOD
On the Table

The first thing we need to take a look at is the food itself. The diet is simple in that we need only to avoid gluten. Things get a little trickier because much of the food produced today is complex, and because gluten has been modified and used in many ways in the processed food industry. To avoid mistaken identities, let's start with these simple guidelines:

- Choose simple and fresh foods over processed foods, which hide more gluten.
- Avoid any ambiguity. Access the ingredient list via a label or the person providing the food. If you can't be sure, skip it.

The ingredient list that follows may seem depressingly long, but remember that only a couple of versions of gluten show up frequently. Many of the other forms of gluten are rare, but you'll need to know them in order to avoid them. Make a copy of this list and keep it in your wallet for grocery shopping. You may want to reduce it on the copier and have it laminated for longevity.

Ingredients to Avoid

Baking powder *	Graham flour	Semolina
Barley	Greunkern	Soy sauce*
Bulgar	HVP* and HPP*	Spelt (dinkel)
Couscous	Kamut	Triticale
Dextrin*	Malt	TVP*
Dinkel (spelt)	Malt flavoring	Wheat bran
Durum wheat	Malt syrup	Wheat flour
Farina	Mir	Wheat germ
Flour	Modified starch*	Wheat starch
Frik	Oats*	
Gluten	Rye	
Gluten flour	Seitan	

Foods marked with an asterisk have the potential for gluten contamination. See page 66 for details on how to contact the manufacturer for more information on the exact derivatives of the ingredient in question.

Starch

Some foods list "starch" as part of their makeup. If the origin of the starch is not clear (e.g., corn, potato, or wheat) it's best to avoid the product altogether.

Soy sauce

Soy sauce is a food that may or may not contain wheat. If you're looking at a product that lists soy sauce as an ingredient but does not list the ingredients of the soy sauce itself, you should avoid the product until you can find out more.

Controversy

Chances are, you've come across some contradictory information regarding the gluten-free diet. There are many associations worldwide and, unfortunately, all do not agree on the foods a celiac should avoid. Books published in different regions or countries as well as information published on the Internet dictate a different version of the diet. But all agree that the celiac diet must not contain:

- Wheat
- Rye

- Barley
- Spelt
- Kamut
- Triticale

To complicate matters further, there is more than one reason for the controversy behind certain foods. Some are concerned about contamination at the milling stage of food production; others fear the consequences of farmers growing wheat crops near or on the same soil as what would otherwise be gluten-free grains. And some doctors omit certain grains from the diet they recommend to patients despite the lack of conclusive evidence from the medical community that these grains contain gluten and/or damage the villi. Often this is because they've treated patients who report adverse reactions to the products. Yet it's possible these patients are intolerant of foods other than gluten.

Meanwhile, in Europe the celiac diet is considered "gluten-restricted" rather than gluten-free. Trace amounts of gluten in a product are permissible; in other words, food products can still contain a minute amount of gluten and be marketed to those on the celiac diet.

Distilled alcohol

Research concludes that the process of distillation leaves the end product free of any traces of gluten even if the grains from which the product was produced contained gluten. *This makes vinegar and vanilla extract gluten-free as well.* (See chapter 10 for more details.)

European Exceptions

The following items are permissible under European standards, but because of the trace amounts of gluten they may contain, are not considered a permissible part of the gluten-free diet in North America:

Oats

Oats do not contain gluten. Although permitted in European countries, we don't promote oats in the North American gluten-free diet because there are some similarities between the makeup of oats and other gluten-containing grains. Some doctors feel there has been a lack of comprehensive research proving that they are indeed safe. In addition, chances of contamination are high, since the milling facilities used to process oats are often the same ones used to process wheat.

Wheat starch

Separating the starch from the other parts of the wheat makes wheat starch. In theory, this process should eliminate gluten; however, trace elements of the gluten may still be present in the starch. Again, wheat starch is permitted in European countries where more allowance is given to the presence of traces of gluten.

It's in the Bag

So now that we're clear on what to avoid, we need to learn which foods are most likely to pose a problem. Obviously, we need to steer clear of conventional breads, cookies, and cakes. However, it's not that clear-cut. Once you start reading those labels, you'll be appalled to learn that forms of gluten can surface in highly unlikely places.

My own life is a case in point. One evening, a friend dropped by with a variety of potato chips for us to nosh on while watching a movie. Upon arrival of the kettle-cooked mesquite chips, the plain ones were abandoned on the kitchen counter. I ripped the bag open and got down to business. Yet after devouring what the manufacturer proclaimed to be seven "servings," I had a wave of curiosity. *What exactly was "mesquite"?*

After perusing the ingredient list, I still can't tell you what that flavor is exactly. Actually, within milliseconds I didn't really care anymore. The ingredients might as well have read arsenic, for they included both wheat flour and malt powder. I think I stopped breathing momentarily. I was in absolute shock. What were *those* things doing in a bag of chips?

There's a big lesson here. I had become overconfident in my ingredient intelligence. Potato chips didn't contain gluten. That was that. I vowed that night to read labels again—at least every time I tried something new. And as you can see I made it through the night. I guess I needed a reminder that even a veteran like me can fall into a trench.

Anything processed requires scrutiny; however, watch the following items in particular for gluten-containing ingredients:

Bouillon cubes	Frozen french fries
Breakfast cereal	Gravy mixes
Candies	Hot chocolate
Canned soups or soup mixes	Ice cream & Popsicles
Chocolate bars	Instant coffee & tea
Chocolate milk	Licorice

Pie fillings	Seasoned chips and snack
Prepared mustard	foods
Processed cheese products	Seasoning mixes
Processed dairy products	Soy milk & rice milk
Processed meats	
Salad dressings	
Seasoned nuts	

Keep in mind, too, that ingredients change. Up until a year ago, I used to be able to buy a brand of chocolate bar. One day I stopped to read the ingredients (unfortunately, *after* I had bought the thing!) only to find that nuzzled amongst the regular ingredients was the offending five-letter word. But better late than never; at least I didn't make myself sick. Next time I'll save my money *and* my health by reading the label first.

Sneaky Gluten

It's not only your food that you need to be watching. Other places where gluten could be making you sick include:

Stamps and envelopes

Use a damp sponge to moisten stamps and the adhesive on envelopes. In many cases, the glue used in your stationary contains gluten.

Playdough, modeling clay, finger paints, and glue

Find out more about these products at home and in your child's school or daycare. *You* might not be eating glue with a spoon, but I distinctly remember what playdough and glue taste like.

Drugs

Ask your pharmacist to check them out on the computer. Pharmacists can access all sorts of information on over-the-counter drugs as well as those available by prescription. Ironically, those antacids you're popping for heartburn could be causing more serious problems, so consider walking them from the candy display to the pharmacist's counter before ingesting.

Vitamins

Buy supplements that clearly state they are gluten-free. These pills and capsules can also include gluten as part of their list of "non-medicinal ingredients." Although they rarely spell out what they *do* include, many product labels will let you know the product doesn't contain gluten, yeast, lactose, corn, or soy, as they are common allergens.

Manufacturing facilities

Inquire about how your food is made. Production lines sometimes dust conveyer belts with flour so that products like candies and chocolate bars don't stick. And products like french fries may be dusted with flour to prevent them from sticking together. But because this flour is not considered an ingredient, the manufacturer is not required to list it on the packaging. (Your local Celiac Association may have already done this homework for you. Check to see if there is a list.)

Toiletries

Watch for reactions to topical products, because what's in your bathroom may be making you sick, too. I didn't believe this myself until I used my friend's wheat germ shampoo. Twelve hours later my scalp was burning and inflamed! If you think you might be having a reaction from a product you're using, contact the manufacturer. Or try taking a break from that particular product and see if your symptoms disappear. Some of the offenders include talcum powder, shampoo, toothpaste, body lotion, lipstick, perfumes, and denture adhesive.

Contamination

Finally, you need to concern yourself with not just the food itself, but the environment in which that food is prepared. If you're following your diet rigorously and still feeling "off," take a closer look at some of the foods you're eating, and look beyond the listed ingredients on the package. Consider all the stages involved in your dinner's journey from manufacturer to plate. These may include various stages of processing, and may have you questioning whether or not the food's production facility produces gluten-laden items with the same machinery as, or in close proximity to, the food you had considered "safe."

In your kitchen at home (or anywhere else you may be eating), take a look at some of the places gluten contamination might occur. You may want to pay special attention to the following:

- Cutting boards
- Knives that leave crumbs in condiments and in the butter dish
- Toaster

- Breadbox and cupboards where bread is stored
- Countertop
- Pots and pans
- Barbecue grill
- Cooking utensils
- Pasta strainer
- Fridge racks that may collect crumbs

In some households, separate equipment is used to avoid problems. At minimum, ensure that surfaces and tools (especially things like pasta strainers) are kept very clean. If you share, use common sense and strain the rice pasta before straining the wheat pasta, and scrub the strainer spotless afterwards. As for toasters, it's best to opt for the toaster oven variety since these are easier to keep clean (the horizontal racks accumulate fewer crumbs, and can be wiped off before toasting "free" bread). Just try to be conscientious rather than paranoid—which isn't healthy either! In no time it will become second nature to consider these things.

Sore Tummies

By following our diet, we can alleviate the nasty symptoms that haunt the celiac. However, on occasion we may still find ourselves in a state of discomfort—felt anywhere between the stomach and the bowels of our beings. To combat this, here are a few natural remedies adept at calming rough seas. It should go without saying that should symptoms persist, get to the doctor's office!

There are many herbs available that claim to help with intestinal troubles. I would advise you to enlist the help of a registered health care professional (like a naturopathic doctor) to help you concoct such remedies. Not knowing what you're doing could cause you more harm than good. I have found the following remedies to be safe, uncomplicated, and readily available.

Teas

Peppermint

Alleviates nausea, dizziness, sore stomach, and gas. Buy teabags or use fresh or dried peppermint on the stove and strain it.

Chamomile

Relieves tension and soothes sore stomachs. Chamomile also works well in combination with peppermint. The bedtime herbal teas on the market are often made of a combination of these two.

Ginger

Eases nausea and aids in digestion. You'll find ginger root in the produce department of the grocery store. Simply slice or grate some up and pour hot water over it (if you rinse it, there's no need to peel). If you don't have any root on hand you can use ground, but the fresh is much nicer. Try this with honey. I drink it every day—with or without medicinal need.

Cinnamon

Helps to slow down or stop diarrhea. Pour boiling water over a teaspoon of ground cinnamon in a mug, or boil water on the stove with whole cinnamon sticks.

Fennel

Relieves gas and bloating. Pour boiling water over a teaspoon of fennel seeds in a mug. They'll sink to the bottom so you don't need to strain it.

Hot water with fresh squeezed lemon

Stimulates and cleanses your system in the morning.

Other Aids

Breathing

Take a moment to relax before starting to eat. This tells the body to change gears. If you're harried, your energy will go towards tasks other than digestion, and eating in a rush is one of the major causes of indigestion.

Chewing

Chew thoroughly. This sounds a bit tongue-in-cheek, but digestion starts in the mouth. If you don't chew your food properly before swallowing it, the stomach has a lot more work to do.

Water

Drink tepid water between meals. It helps to alleviate constipation and aids in flushing out illness in the body. Drink it between meals rather than in large doses with meals as the liquids only dilute your digestive enzymes. Try drinking it cool or at room temperature because very cold liquids are much harder on your stomach.

Applesauce and cinnamon

Both the pectin (in the apples) and the cinnamon help to bind what's in your system, and slow down diarrhea. Keep some in the house for times of need.

Lemon

Eat a whole lemon (you can cut it up and sprinkle it with sugar if you find it intolerably sour). This is a traditional remedy that I learned in Italy to alleviate diarrhea.

Acidophilus

Your intestinal tract is full of both healthy and unhealthy bacteria, and it's important to keep the two balanced for normal functioning. Acidophilus is healthy bacteria, just like the bacteria naturally present in your system. Chances are, if you're suffering from diarrhea, both the good and bad bacteria are being flushed out of your system. Acidophilus will build the healthy bacteria back up and help you fight off infection. If you can tolerate lactose, have a yogurt; otherwise, take acidophilus capsules, which are available at your health food store or herbalist.

Aromatic seeds

These prevent gas, and are used in India after meals to aid in digestion and freshen the breath. Chew on fennel, caraway, and anise seeds as they do in India, or make them into a tea like the fennel tea described above.

For years, my stomach was a mess—despite my strict adherence to a gluten-free diet. Sadly, sometimes there are other foods that can upset our stomachs almost as much as a box of forbidden donuts, something I had to come to terms with when I realized I was lactose intolerant. Years later, when my symptoms continued to persist, I learned that mushrooms, certain fruits, and anything containing yeast or moulds were also causing my stomach to bloat.

Teas, seeds, and applesauce are quick fixes. Everyone feels "off" sometimes. However, if you feel like you're perpetually seeking out these comforts, write up a diet diary describing how your body feels after eating certain foods (see chapter 3 for details). Then, if you still can't make sense of what in your diet is troubling you, bring along your diary the next time you visit your health care provider. Together, you can review your concerns, and come up with some answers.

Understanding what you can and cannot eat is important, but your new "limitations" may bring up a host of new feelings as well. Chapter 3 will help you to identify and work through these feelings, so that eventually, you'll come to regard your new diet with a sense of adventure rather than resentment.

3
THE FEELINGS
It Takes Guts

Since we cannot change reality, let us change the eyes which see reality.

—*Nikos Kazantzakis*

Food for Thought

Life revolves around food, since we require sustenance to keep us alive. Now that we know what not to eat, we shouldn't have any problem staying alive. The challenge is to create a life that's worth living, despite the restrictions we face.

I used to get so sick of hearing, "Oh you poor thing! What *do* you eat?" You'll occasionally bump into these melodramatic pastry-poppers at cocktail parties, but today, you're more likely to hear someone say something like, "Gluten intolerance right? My nephew has that."

Our social lives are largely arranged around food and drink. Initially, people will probably feel badly for eating the bread on the table in front of you. They'll be afraid to invite you to their home for a meal, and they won't have a clue as to how to address your needs until you spell it all out for them. Some stupid and insensitive things will be said and done.

Acknowledge that it might take some time to accept change. Go through the feelings as they surface rather than stuffing them down both literally and figuratively. As the therapists will tell you, moving through your negative emotions really is the best way of getting over them.

Take a look at just how many negative feelings and emotions we're capable of. Maybe you find yourself feeling:

Abandoned
Aggressive
Agitated
Altered
Angry
Annoyed
Anxious
Argumentative
Awkward
Bitter
Bored
Burdened
Challenged
Cautious
Cheated
Cold
Complaining
Condemned
Confused
Conspicuous
Crushed
Childish
Cynical
Defeated
Defensive
Demanding
Dependent
Depressed
Desolate
Despondent
Destructive
Different
Diminished
Disappointed
Discontented
Dissatisfied
Distraught

Dull
Emotional
Enraged
Envious
Exhausted
Fearful
Flustered
Frantic
Frightened
Frustrated
Fussy
Gloomy
Guilty
Hateful
High-strung
Horrible
Hostile
Humorless
Hurt
Hysterical
Ignored
Immature
Impatient
Infantile
Infuriated
Intolerant
Irritable
Irritated
Isolated
Jealous
Left out
Lonely
Longing
Low
Mad
Meek
Melancholy

Miserable
Moody
Nagging
Nervous
Obsessed
Odd
Overwhelmed
Pained
Panicked
Peculiar
Persecuted
Pessimistic
Petrified
Pitiful
Preoccupied
Quarrelsome
Quiet
Resentful
Rigid
Rude
Sad
Scared
Screwed up
Self-centered
Self-pitying
Sorrowful
Suffering
Sulky
Tempted
Tense
Terrified
Threatened
Thwarted
Touchy
Trapped
Troubled
Uneasy

Unstable	Wary	Whiny
Violent	Weak	Withdrawn
Vulnerable	Weepy	Worried

When I look at this long list, I realize that over the years I've experienced almost every feeling on it in various food-related situations. But the moments when I'm freaked out by the need to have that piece of pecan pie are always about something much bigger than dessert. Being surrounded by foods that make you sick can "bring up"—if you'll pardon the pun—all kinds of issues, particularly when you want to eat and there appears to be nothing around that's safe for you.

If you find yourself overwhelmed or confused by your emotions, keep a journal. Start by describing in detail how you were feeling before your diagnosis. As emotions related to your new lifestyle hit you, record them. Write about discoveries at restaurants, in the kitchen, or on shopping trips. And don't forget to write about the benefits you're reaping from this healthier way of living, too. There *will* come a point of acceptance, which will bring long periods of calm and satisfaction. This journal will be a reminder of the journey you have made so far, and will provide a way of putting it all back into perspective when you've had a rough day.

Another important step to help you get started is a diet diary. This is not an exercise in how to be a control freak, but rather a way of showing you exactly how you're sustaining yourself. You might be very surprised at just how much you eat of one food, and perhaps also what you might completely lack from a nutritional standpoint. Keep a chart on your refrigerator or in a notebook (depending on your lifestyle and your need for privacy). Record what you eat for at least two weeks to get a good overview of your typical diet. What I'm hoping you'll see here is where you need to expand your repertoire, where you're lacking variety, or where something you're ingesting is throwing you off. Try to do this exercise and take a look for yourself—I bet you'll be surprised by what you find.

Making a Diet Diary

1. Make a chart on a single page for the week. This way you can see the week as a whole.
2. Turn the paper sideways and write the days of the week across the top.
3. Write breakfast, lunch, and dinner down the left side of the page.

4. Draw lines making a square for you to record each meal in. Make them big enough to record snacks between meals and after dinner.
5. Create more than one, or make blank copies for the weeks that follow.
6. Record everything that you eat and drink throughout the day.
7. Turn the page over, and on the back record how you felt—physically and emotionally—on each day. Was there a particular food situation you found problematic?

Once you have a better idea of what it is you're eating, you'll be able to see where your nutritional deficiencies are, as well as where boredom might be getting you down. What I'm hoping is that by using these tools you'll begin to feel empowered. And once you acknowledge that you're making a *choice* to feel healthy by not eating that apple pie, you're less likely to resent not being able to eat it. You may not be convinced today, but in a very short time you won't believe how little that apple pie is going to mean to you!

Family Affairs

If you live with others, you'll need to sit down with them to discuss your new diet, and how the change will affect the rest of the tribe. There are some issues that are best dealt with early to avoid resentment and flare-ups.

Questions for the Person with Restrictions

- How do you feel about having the temptation of restricted foods in the house?
- Which foods would be most difficult for you to have around?
- What do you need from the other members of the family to make things easier?

Questions for the Caregiver or Meal Provider

- What meals are easily adaptable to the new diet?
- How often do you want to make two different versions of a meal?
- Will you make two pots of pasta, or will everyone eat the "free" version?
- If you are both the meal provider and the one with the new diet, how do you feel about preparing foods that make you sick?

Questions for the Rest of the Family

- What would other members of the family miss most if the household went "free"?
- Would they be agreeable to keeping the foods that cause the most angst (for you) out of the house?

Every family dynamic is different. There may be some resentment about the fact that there won't be any Oreo cookies in the cupboard now that Sally can't eat them. Remember that everyone is going to need some empathy. You may decide to change just one person's diet. If it's you, then that is your decision; but if it's your child's, try to keep them feeling as included as possible at home.

Given the fact that there are so many different dishes available to us on this earth, there's absolutely no reason you should be bored on a "free" diet. Your family can have an exciting selection of foods from around the world that are as easy to prepare as anything else you used to serve. The trick is to learn how to whip up meals that are fast and easy to make from scratch; but we'll get into that later. For now, remember that it's important to remain flexible until everyone in your household has had a chance to get used to things. If you're the one with the new diet and are also the family chef, you might at first try making separate meals for yourself until you get used to the idea that no one need feel deprived about being asked to eat like you do. Or you might want to insist that everyone eat what you're eating. If your attitude changes as time goes on, respect your feelings. Keep in mind that it's only food. No matter how you're handling it, you're probably a lot more fun to be around now that you're not sick anymore.

Growing Pains

I don't actually remember meeting other children with "lunch pail issues." There may have been a kid allergic to strawberries one year, though I could just be fantasizing. I do recall my classmates making funny faces at my rice cakes and the nasty little dry and crumbly sandwiches I tried to wolf down as fast as I could. I also remember yearning for the prepackaged chemical-tasting goodies that were the rage of my juvenile generation.

I recently picked up a cookbook published in Britain in the early '70s that contained a number of suggestions on how to raise a child with celiac disease. The author of the book stressed that the child should not be allowed to feel sorry for him or herself, and that the rest of the family should behave as if his or her restrictions were no big deal. But this attitude tells the child that:

- She has to toughen up
- Life is not fair—too bad
- He is not worth special attention
- She should in no way inconvenience you

However, if you go to the other extreme and are uptight and rigid, your child may believe that:

- You don't trust him
- You don't trust anyone
- She is very fragile
- He could die at any moment
- Every illness she gets is a result of celiac or food allergies
- He is very different from everyone else
- She makes your life stressful

Being in a bad mood at home signaled to my mother that I had eaten gluten. Unfortunately, both of us came to associate my being in a bad mood with my being "bad"—which, of course, just wasn't the case. It's important not to make a child feel like a delinquent for having made a mistake. Sometimes she'll push the envelope, as all children do. Believe that if your child has eaten something bad there will be punishment enough. If she succumbs to the temptation of a box of Girl Guide Cookies—as I did in grade three—she'll be very sick. Throwing up in the school lobby meant that I was also humiliated. Was the lesson learned? You bet it was.

At some point, *every* kid learns how to ride a two-wheeler. You can't be around every minute to ensure that he doesn't fall, but there are some safety measures that you can take. Visiting with the school principal, day-care supervisor or camp counselor and putting details in writing for them to distribute to all caregivers is a good start. You can also contact your child's teacher and the school nurse directly to voice any concerns and get a better idea of how lunches and snacks are monitored (particularly in the early elementary years). By making direct contact each year you'll also be giving your child's teacher an opportunity to ask questions or share concerns. This can be done discreetly so that the child does not feel singled out. For example, you might tell your child that you've called his teachers to let them know about food intolerances so that he doesn't feel that you've been secretive. Let your child know you care, and that you're working together as a team.

Some issues you may want to raise can be communicated in the following ways:

- Provide a written list of what a teacher will need to know for your child's file (your support group will likely have a pamphlet).
- Explain your child's possible need for special (and discreet) bathroom privileges.
- Find out if there is a snack time where cookies are distributed, and if so provide the teacher with a box of safe biscuits to keep on hand.
- Request that you be notified when the school is offering food or hosting events such as hot dog days or bake sales.
- Talk about the hidden dangers of playdough and glue (which very young children will eat).
- Advise on how you would like your child to be addressed should a teacher find him or her eating something that isn't safe—knowingly or otherwise.
- Ask your child if there are any other concerns she'd like you to discuss with a teacher that she may not be comfortable with.
- Let the school know how you can be reached, should someone need to discuss things further.

Nowadays many schools have adopted a "no peanut butter in school" policy due to the fatal results for children allergic to nuts. As a parent, you can make a difference. Why not suggest that the school your child attends acknowledge and discuss with its students other food-related illnesses? Let them know that while these are normal, they can also be very serious. If everyone is comfortable and understands the situation, the intolerant child will feel less like a freak of nature. Ignorance amongst children is often a cause of great cruelty. When classmates understand, they feel more connected to the situation, and are less likely to make it a big deal. In fact, they're also far more likely to become involved, and to start looking out for one another.

Encouraging your child to be involved in his or her self-care is important for self-esteem. When the child is old enough, encourage him or her to talk about needs, ask questions, and express concerns. Feeling empowered rather than smothered will result in better decisions all around.

Most of *my* cheating experiences happened at an age when I felt that the world was out to control me. This is normal for an adolescent. Indeed, sometimes your desire to look out for your teenager will not be read as caring, but as controlling. The best way to keep on top of a situation over which you have little control is to schedule a yearly visit with your teenager's specialist. Go along, but stay in the waiting area for the duration of the appointment. Give your kid an opportunity to speak with someone objective. Rest assured, you'll get your answers along with the test results. And if the tests show that your child has strayed, save the sermon. Leave it to the doctor to remind him or her of the consequences of poor choices. At 16, my gastro gave me a terrifying speech, but if it had come from my mother, it wouldn't have had the same impact.

Trying to function in an adult world can be very overwhelming. It's a time of assessing limits and taking risks. Teenagers typically experiment with drinking, smoking, and a variety of other dangerous habits that they know are very bad for them. All the preaching in the world won't keep most teenagers from doing what they see their friends doing, because dying of lung cancer just isn't an issue. And the fact that the symptoms of celiac disease often go into a form of remission during adolescence also makes it easier to blow off a warning.

What you can do is help your child learn how to make smart choices. And, while you're at it, why not encourage the kids to hang out at *your* house on Friday night? Having plenty of "free" snacks around to munch on will make everyone feel welcome, and will greatly reduce the urge to just order pizza.

Coping skills are not going to come automatically. I can tell you it's going to be just fine, but you have to arrive at that place on your own to really believe it. Chapter 4 is about getting there and—while you're at it—finding some new friends and healthy support.

4

THE SUPPORT

Strength in Numbers

Getting Help

When I was diagnosed with celiac disease, my support group consisted of my mother. In 1973, my mother trekked out to *her* support group, which was a very small gathering of women who met two hours away from where we lived. Today, I'm a member of a local chapter that serves well over a thousand members, and I'm convinced that there's no need to go at this alone. You wouldn't believe the resources and support that are available to you.

Health Care Professionals

Family practitioner/Gastroenterologist

Both your family practitioner and your gastroenterologist should be conferred with first regarding any health concerns you may have. If you're suffering and can't trace the culprit, talk to a professional. You may be overlooking a hazardous habit.

Dietitian

A registered dietitian is often the first person you're put in contact with after diagnosis. Unfortunately, at the time of diagnosis, it's unlikely that you knew all of the questions and concerns that were going to come up.

This visit doesn't have to be a one-shot deal. Ask your doctor for a referral for a follow-up visit after you've been following the diet for six months or so. It's a good idea to keep a diet diary for a week or so before a follow-up visit. That way, your dietitian can adequately review just how you've been sustaining yourself, since you may, for example, be deficient in certain vitamins and minerals.

Naturopath

I'm not about to recommend naturopathic doctors in lieu of traditional medical practitioners. Celiac disease is a disorder that requires the attention of a gastroenterologist. Naturopaths are, however, a great source of guidance in matters of overall health. Licensed naturopathic doctors have at least seven years of training in basic medical sciences such as anatomy, physiology, immunology, pathology, and pharmacology. They also gain experience in the following naturopathic modalities: clinical nutrition, homeopathy, Oriental medicine and acupuncture, botanical medicine, hydrotherapy, bodywork, stress management, and lifestyle counseling. There are six accredited schools in North America (five in the US and one in Canada), and to graduate, students must pass a board exam called NPLEX. Not every state and province is regulated, however, so it's wise to check credentials.

An N.D. will help you explore the relationship between your body, mind, and spirit, and will assist you on the road to good health through a combination of gentle, non-invasive techniques that work with your body's own healing abilities. Naturopathic doctors promote preventative medicine as the best means of achieving optimal health.

Books on Celiac Disease and Related Issues

To learn more about issues that relate directly to your health condition, take a look at the following:

Good Food, Gluten Free
Hilda Cherry Hills
Keats Publishing, Inc., 1976

The New Healing Yourself
Joy Gardner
Crossing Press, 1989

For anecdotal stories from other celiacs, take a look at:

No Grain, No Pain
Shirley Marie Hartung, 2000
Available via: *www.edible-options.com*

For a more "by the books" physician-oriented dietary resource and manufacturer's guide, see:

Gluten-free Diet: A Comprehensive Resource Guide
Shelley Case B.Sc., R.D.
Case Nutritional Consulting, 2005
Available via: *www.glutenfreediet.ca*

Visit your local library and get on the computer system that links with other branches in your area. Try using the search terms "celiac" or "gluten-free" to see what they have kicking around. You may come across some terrific books that are no longer in print.

Celiac Associations

Go to the meetings! Rubbing shoulders with fellow dietary invalids is good for your mental health. The cost of membership is well worth it even if you only use association newsletters for new recipes, product lists, and keeping abreast of recent research. These associations are without a doubt the best resource available to a gluten-intolerant. Remember, too, that support groups depend on volunteers, and those volunteers are regular people like you and me. If you have the inclination to contact manufacturers yourself, or if you simply enjoy helping others, you're probably just the kind of person your local chapter needs. And you'll learn all kinds of important information that will help your own cause while you assist and support others.

The following is a list of the larger associations in North America. In nearly every major city and in almost every state and province, there are also smaller local chapters. Contact one of these groups to find out the regional chapter that's closest to where you live.

American Celiac Association
Dietary Support Coalition
58 Musano Court
West Orange, NJ 07052
201 325 8837

Canadian Celiac Association
5170 Dixie Road, Suite 204
Mississauga, ON L4W 1E3
905 507 6208
800 363 7296

Celiac Sprue Association
P.O. Box 31700
Omaha, NE 68131-0700
402 558 0600

The Gluten Intolerance
Group of North America, Inc.
P.O. Box 23053
Seattle, WA 98102-0353
206 325 6980

Celiac Disease Foundation
13251 Ventura Boulevard, Suite 3
Studio City, CA 91604-1838
818 990 2354

Publications Related to Celiac Disease

Regular newsletters are available through membership in the support groups listed above. You may also want to check out the following periodicals, which are published regularly and made available through a variety of independent sources.

Living Without Magazine
PO Box 2126
Northbrook, IL 60065
847 480 8810
www.livingwithout.com

Gluten-Free Living
Published quarterly
19A Broadway
Hawthorn, NY 10532
914 741 5420
www.glutenfreeliving.com
info@glutenfreeliving.com

The Gluten-Free
Baker Newsletter
by Sandra Leonard
361 Cherrywood Dr.
Fairborn, OH 45324-4012
513 878 3221
thebaker@CRIS.COM

Friends

What are they for? Ask people to keep their eyes open in the grocery or health food stores, as well as for magazine or newspaper articles they might come across. You can also ask them to check out menus for a variety of gluten-free foods when they go out for dinner. I'm not suggesting that your friends have nothing better to do, but if they notice a menu with a great selection of rice dishes, for example, let them know that you'd appreciate the info. The point here is that by recruiting more people to keep their eyes open for you, you'll be exposed to more options. Then, next time someone suggests that the group go out for dinner, you can offer up a selection of places that you know in advance will work for you.

Strangers

Forget what your mother told you. Talk to the people you see perusing the gluten-free items in health food stores. If someone is buying rice bread and cookies, I will often strike up a conversation. I like to ask what their favorite brands are and why. You might make some new friends!

The Internet

Speaking of strangers, why not connect with fellow gluten-intolerant people on other continents? There's a lot of information floating around out there, but do keep in mind that not all of it is qualified and monitored. There are hundreds of sites you can land on if you begin your search with the word "celiac." I find that the Internet can get overwhelming, so I've listed what I consider to be some of the better-quality sites by category. Use what you find with discretion, and remember to have some fun!

National Celiac Association and Support Groups

Celiac Sprue Association, United States of America, Inc.
www.csaceliacs.org

The Gluten Intolerance Group (GIG)
www.gluten.net

Celiac Disease Foundation
www.celiac.org

The Canadian Celiac Association
www.celiac.ca

Celiac Disease and Gluten-Free Diet Support Center
www.celiac.com / www.gluten-free.com

National Foundation for Celiac Awareness
www.celiacawareness.org

Celiac Forums
www.celiacforums.com

Celiac Sprue Research Foundation
www.celiacsprue.org

Other Related Associations

National Digestive Diseases Information Clearinghouse
www.niddk.nih.gov, search: celiac

Mayo Clinic, Health Oasis
www.mayoclinic.com

The Enabling Support Foundation
www.enabling.org/ia/celiac/

University Celiac Sites

Columbia University
www.cumc.columbia.edu/dept/medicine

Simon Fraser University
www.sfu.ca/~jfremont/celiac.html

University of Maryland, Center for Celiac Research
www.celiaccenter.org

St.Johns University, New York
(This is an interactive website that brings together gluten-intolerant
people from around the world.)
listserv@maelstrom.stjohns.edu

Shopping

Many manufacturers and grain wholesalers will mail food to you anywhere on the continent. For those who live in big cities, this may not
seem like such an exciting option, but in rural areas mail order can be a
godsend. Check out these shopping sites on the Internet:

The Gluten-Free Pantry
www.glutenfree.com

Distributor of EnerG foods
www.liv-n-well.com

Gluten Solutions
www.glutensolutions.com

Panne Rizo Bakery
www.pannerizo.com

The Gluten-Free Mall
www.glutenfreemall.com

El Peto Products Limited
www.elpeto.com

Kinnikinnick Bakery
www.kinnikinnick.com

Recipes

Recipes from the
Gluten-Free Pantry
www.glutenfree.com/recipes.html

Celiacs, Inc.
www.e-celiacs.org

The Gluten Free Kitchen
gfkitchen.server101.com

Children

North American Society for Pediatric
Gastroenterology and Nutrition
www.naspgn.org

Travel

The Celiac Travel Pages
www.clanthompson.com

CeliacTravel.com
www.celiactravel.com

Bob & Ruth's Gluten-Free Dining & Travel Club
www.bobandruths.com

So you can see you're not alone. Once you start meeting other celiac patients you'll feel an instant bond, like meeting some distant relative for the first time. (Nothing brings people together like their food!) Now that you're educated, relaxed, and connected, it's time to spring to action— and there's no better place to start pulling it all together than your own kitchen.

5
THE SET UP
Cupboard Love

Clarity Begins at Home

Many of us look to the kitchen for more than just nourishment. We stroll in looking for comfort and pleasure. But there's not a lot of comfort in opening up the cupboards only to find tasty foods that you don't get along with anymore. We need to create a place where the "comforts of home" await.

What follows are some simple ways of working in your space. The idea is to set things up so that all members of the household are responsible for keeping the kitchen safe. Hopefully you've discussed this as a family, because you'll need to set some boundaries. As some things in the kitchen are inaccessible to you, you should feel entitled to a space that's equally inaccessible to the others.

Start by taking a look in the cupboards. First, empty everything out and put it into two piles. One is for members of the family unaffected by toxic culprits. The other pile is what's safe for you to eat. This means that the cans of soup, dehydrated scalloped potato mix, pasta, coatings, cake mixes, and chocolate chip cookies all go into one pile and the chickpeas and canned corn go into another. Admittedly, you won't find a lot of comfort in a can of chickpeas. For now, however, you're just going to have to trust me.

If you're sharing a home with people who tolerate gluten, you may do things differently than you would for an entirely "free" household.

Plan A

Find some bags or a box. Load all offending products into them and take them to a neighbor or local food bank. Take the opportunity to wipe out your cupboards. Make them nice and clean. This is a fresh start. And be patient—soon you'll discover so many tasty and exciting new foods that you'll run out of cupboard space.

Plan B

Your cupboards are bare and all the food they once contained is sitting in two piles on the counter. Clean the shelves off for your fresh start. Now step back and decide which shelf you want for your own (you get first choice). Do you want a shelf out of the way so that the other family members don't automatically reach for your "free" cookies? If you're trying to accommodate more than one diet, I suggest you create the following three separate sections.

The gluten shelf

Here you'll sector off all the foods you don't want to deal with anymore. This food will be what other members of the household can prepare when you're not around, or what might go into their bagged lunches, etc.

The neutral shelf

Here you'll put food that anyone can eat at any time. This shelf has friendly products for everyone on it. If you don't mind sharing some of your "free" treats with other members of the family, you can put some of those here, too. Don't be surprised if some of the "free" foods that you're going to find become the family favorites!

The "free" shelf

This is yours alone, because *they* have a shelf and so should you. Fair, if you ask me. This is your stash, and it should be understood that it's as off limits to everyone else as theirs is to you. On this shelf you can keep a stock of rice crackers, cookies, flavored rice cakes, etc., along with all of the new goodies you'll be discovering when you go *shopping*!

The Refrigerator

The refrigerator should be dealt with in a similar way; however, it can be more difficult to isolate sections. Why not take over the crisper drawers as your own? (Most people forget to look in there anyway!) One drawer can contain fun hands-off snacks that should be refrigerated; the other can be filled with things like gluten-free baking supplies and special flours.

Get to know which condiments are off-limits, and sway your family towards the "free" options (of which there are many). If they're stubborn, keep two brands of mustard in the house and make sure that you're never the one to go without. The new rule is: *It's all about you.*

If you're organizing for a child, a great way to arrange food is with a sticker system. This doesn't have to be as tedious as it might sound. Pick a color—let's say red. Buy a package of round red stickers and stick them to everything in the house that's safe for your child to eat. This will make things very clear for the child while he or she is learning which cereals or snacks are safe. This is also especially helpful to babysitters and visitors who are not experienced with your child's diet.

The sticker system can work well for grown-ups, too. If you're extremely sensitive, beware of the contamination possibilities of sharing certain foods. For example, a knife used on whole wheat bread and then dipped into the peanut butter may be enough to make some people quite ill. Why not put a sticker on anything meant to be kept "free"? If you have two jars of peanut butter, the others can stay away from the one with the red dot on the lid. Some families have even adopted a "no knife policy," meaning that everyone shares the same products, but uses a clean spoon to scoop condiments from jars, instead of the knife they use to spread the product. Squeeze bottles eliminate the problem completely.

The transition will be easier if you source out the best "free" versions of the foods your family tends to eat most. For example, if you eat a lot of pasta, load up on corn and rice pasta—and buy the best that you can afford. Ready-made pie crusts for chicken pot pies and pizza shells are available, albeit expensive. Don't scrimp on yourself. In time, it won't feel as ridiculous to spend what it costs for these conveniences, and as you learn about other options, you'll end up reaching for them less often.

On the topic of shopping, you should also learn to keep the freezer stocked up with "free" staples, since it's still not possible to find rice bread at the convenience store. However, don't overdo it with "free" flours, since gluten-free flours have a shorter shelf life than wheat flour. Many have a higher fat content, and go off if kept for too long. I keep mine in the refrigerator in jars that are clearly labeled with date of purchase so I'm sure to use up the oldest first. I also like to keep a variety of flours, as each has distinct properties and flavors. It's best to have just a few cups of those you use most frequently in the fridge at any one time. Keeping them in the freezer is a good idea if the flours are not as readily available where you live and you're forced to buy larger quantities. We'll look more closely at the types of flours available to you in chapter 8.

Generally speaking, if you weren't much of a chef before diagnosis, you might find yourself a little more inclined to make homemade soup now that the variety of what's available to you in a tin is considerably lessened. The good news is that not only will you feel better from the lack of gluten, but you'll also find yourself eating fewer processed foods.

Once you get comfortable with your new eating regime in your own home, it'll start to feel easier to interact with the outside world. Why not throw a dinner party first and show your friends that you can still function socially? Soon it'll be you bringing the best dishes to the potluck!

Cookbooks as Tour Guides

At first you may feel like you want everything to come out of a manual of dos and don'ts, since the idea of living outside the safety zone can be terrifying. Until you get into the groove of this new lifestyle, it's understandable that you may only want to work from specialty cookbooks that cater to those on a "restricted" diet. If you're inclined to bake your own muffins, cakes, and bread, track down the fantastic cookbooks out there by Bette Hagman. Gluten-free baking is a tricky business, and Hagman will save you a lot of grief. "Free" recipes can also be found in books aimed at people with allergies and intolerances.

When you've exhausted these recipes and feel ready to expand your repertoire, you'll know you're also ready to jump back into the mainstream, using your new knowledge to filter out what's safe to eat and which recipes will easily convert. Remember that an omelet never did contain gluten; you don't need a gluten-free cookbook to tell you how to make one.

When you buy a cookbook, think of it as a workbook. Anyone who has experienced baking with flour of the "free" variety will tell you that it's a constant science experiment. You're the scientist, and you can save yourself a lot of trouble by writing a quick note on the page of a recipe once you've given it a shot. For example, "Tastes like drywall!" saves you time and the embarrassment of making it for company. I like to jot comments such as "A little too moist—try with less liquid next time." I might also write things like "Only had one egg and it still worked fine!" I also tend to modify based on what I have in the house, so a banana muffin recipe might read "Used apples and added cinnamon and I liked it better." This is also very helpful if you lend out your book to someone in need (put your name on it!) because the person using it can benefit from your experience.

My favorite recipe books are the ones with the dog-eared corners and the stains on them. My books are also tabbed with Post-it notes for quick reference. When I have time to kick back and relax, I take a book from my collection and a pad of Post-its and mark the recipes that appeal to me. I must admit that I don't bother to tag things that are even remotely complicated or have too many ingredients. I prefer simple, inspirational recipes that contain everyday ingredients that I'm likely to have in the house, and perhaps one interesting new component that I can make a point of shopping for on the week of divine inspiration.

Often when we grocery shop aimlessly, we find ourselves picking up the same ingredients. When it comes to making dinner, we find ourselves preparing the same old foods we know and love. When you're inspired by a new recipe idea, immediately adding the ingredients to your shopping list will help alleviate this problem.

One thing is for sure: you'll become more food obsessed, and you'll also be on constant lookout for new food ideas. I love cooking magazines because they're full of beautiful photos and seasonal recipes. I migrate towards the ones that are focused on a grain group that I can eat—for example, an issue that focuses on regional corn recipes. The only problem with magazines is that they can build up pretty quickly, and when you want to make a dish, you're forced to search through lots of copies and too many advertisements. I suggest that you cut out the recipes you want to keep.

Speaking of issues that focus on a particular grain, you might want to dip into your pocket and treat yourself to a lovely cookbook on rice or potatoes now that you'll be cooking with them more often. And there's no need to avoid any of the terrific pasta cookbooks out there; just remember to substitute lighter and healthier "free" pasta!

The only limitations you have are the ones that you choose. Take a day trip to a mega bookstore and stand in front of the wall with cookbooks piled from floor to ceiling. Remind yourself that you'll never have the time to try everything still available to you on your so-called "limited" diet.

Reading List

There are many books on the market that are written for a gluten- and wheat-free audience. I own a lot more than you'll find on this list. What I've provided here are the ones I consider most useful. Look on the bookshelves of your health food stores as well as regular bookstores. Check your local library for books that may be out of print, and contact your local celiac support group for their list of recommendations, as some smaller publications are only distributed regionally. Finally, don't forget to use the Internet to track down books from all over the planet!

Recommended "Specialty Diet" Cookbooks

The Gluten-Free Gourmet
Bette Hagman
Henry Holt and Company, 1990

The Good Gut Cookbook
Rosemary Stanton
The Gut Foundation
Bay Books, Harper Collins, 1994

More From the Gluten-Free Gourmet
Bette Hagman
Henry Holt and Company, 1993

Full of Beans
Violet Curry, Kay Spicer
Mighton House, 1993

The Gluten-Free Gourmet Cooks Fast and Healthy
Bette Hagman
Henry Holt and Company, 1996

The "No-Gluten" Solution
Pat Cassady Redjou
RAE Publications, 1990
To order this book, contact Pat Redjou c/o
"NO-GLUTEN" SOLUTION
Box 731
Brush Prairie, WA
98606-0731

Wheat-Free Recipes & Menus
Carol Fenster, Ph.D.
Avery/Penguin Group, 2004

The Gluten-Free Gourmet Bakes Bread
Bette Hagman
Henry Holt and Company, 1999

The Sensitive Gourmet: Imaginative Cooking Without Dairy, Wheat or Gluten
Antionette Savill
Thorsons, 1998

*The Everyday Wheat-Free &
Gluten-Free Cookbook*
Michelle Berriedale-Johnson
Key Porter Books, 2000

Freedom from Allergy Cookbook
Ronald Greenberg, M.D.
Angela Nori
Blue Poppy Press, 1996

125 Best Gluten-Free Recipes
Donna Washburn, P.H.Ec. &
& Heather Butt, P.H.Ec.
Robert Rose, 2003

Gluten-Free
Micheal Cox
Fireside/Simon & Schuster,
2000

*The Best Gluten-Free Family
Cookbook*
Donna Washburn, P.H.Ec. &
& Heather Butt, P.H.Ec.
Robert Rose, 2005

Recipe Binders for Overachievers

The old-fashioned way to keep recipes was in a box with neat little index cards. That was before the age of periodical bombardment. Since then, we've also seen a serious shift in attitude towards the running of a household. I have one of those recipe boxes, and I haven't added anything to it in years. Who has time to write out each recipe? Instead, why not try the following? All you need is:

- A binder
- Clear plastic pockets with punched holes for binders
- Colored dividers with tabs for binders
- A pair of scissors

If something looks interesting, save it. There's nothing to transcribe and no magazines to clutter up your home. What's more, you can put everything in this binder: recipes from friends, celiac newsletters, tips you find, even inspiring pictures. To make things easier to find, organize and separate the recipes by food type. Now you'll have all your recipes in one place—your resource/scrapbook.

The best part about this system is that it evolves as you do. If you try something and you don't like it, simply remove it from its plastic sheet to make room for something else. You don't run out of room; you simply add pages. Eventually, you may have to buy a bigger binder, or split desserts from mains and put them into separate binders—whatever works for you.

Next time you try a new recipe from one of your cookbooks and it turns out well, write the name, source, and page number on the colored divider in your binder. For example:

Potato dumplings   *ABC Cooking*   *Page 42*

Write this on the divider page that coincides with the starch, which in this case would be the divider for potato recipes. Now when you want to make a potato dish, you have a list of successes on the first page, and lots of new inspirational ideas in the plastic pouches that follow. On nights when you're feeling less inspired, why not ask another family member to choose something from your binder and have *them* make it for you?

Now that you're organized, it's time to fill those cupboards. Armed with the right information about what to avoid, you'll feel a lot more confident when you finally hit the grocery store. So, get your pen and paper ready—you're about to create a better gluten-free list than you ever thought possible.

6

THE PROVISIONS

Shop Without Dropping

Touring the Aisles

I love grocery shopping. I'm aware, of course, that I'm an exception when I look at all the sour faces waiting in the checkout line. Whether you enjoy the supermarket or not, you can benefit from getting to know your grocery store more intimately. If you take the time to peruse and map out each aisle, you'll know where all the great gluten-free products are and which rows to skip altogether.

Nobody's going to tell you not to check out the bakery section. That's the place where on occasion you'll find a styrofoam tray with suspicious pink meringues covered in colored sprinkles. But remember that even the innocent-looking coconut macaroons usually contain gluten. After a couple of brave or naive attempts to find something edible in the bakery, my guess is that you'll realize your time is better spent elsewhere.

The butcher section is generally pretty safe if you're buying undressed or unadulterated meat or fish. The same *cannot* be said for the deli. Some processed meats, including cold cuts and patés, are not wheat- or gluten-free. Insist that the person behind the counter pull out the package where the ingredients are listed. Ask that your cold cuts be cut from that package, and not be taken out of the precut selection in the display counter where you don't really know what you're getting. Don't be afraid to ask them to clean the blade before slicing your meat. As for sausages and wieners, don't buy anything that doesn't come with a list of ingredients. Remember that pre-basted chickens and turkeys are "processed foods" to an extent. The less adulterated food is, the less likely it will be contaminated. Veggie burgers are almost always held together with gluten. If you're looking for a meat substitute, try bean or tofu patties from the health food store instead.

The dairy section of the grocery store has plenty of items that are "free" if you can tolerate lactose. Watch out for gluten in processed cheese products like spreads and sauces. This is not necessarily the case today, but the ingredients listed on the packaging never indicate what these "cultures" are grown from. If you love this kind of cheese, it would be worth a call to the distributor of the products. As for ice cream, skip anything with cookies or dough in it for sure, and read the labels of whatever else you're considering. The same goes for chocolate popsicles, flavored yogurts, and chip dips.

Take the time to go through all the canned soups, the processed rice or potato packages, the sauce mixes, the frozen dinners, etc. You'll save yourself a great deal of time in the long run knowing what you *can* reach for. There are scalloped potato and rice mixes that are "free." However, the ingredients are often sketchy on the packaging. I wouldn't use the product without a phone call to the manufacturer first. I personally try to avoid as many of these processed products as possible, but I do keep a few cans of "free" soup in the cupboard as emergency rations.

I met a man at one of our Celiac Association meetings who takes his cell phone into the grocery store and actually calls the manufacturers while he shops. This is, of course, much easier when there's a 1-800 number on the label of the product in question. Your local Celiac Association chapter is likely to have done a lot of investigative work on which brands of processed foods are gluten-free. Beware of trusting ingredient lists for products made available in other geographic regions than the one you live in. One product may be made differently in different factories. A breakfast cereal could be gluten-free in America. The same cereal made in Canada could have malt in it.

There seems to be a grocery store evolution taking place. The new superstores may not have the charm of the small local grocer, but they do have an appeal all their own. The best part about these mammoth theme park groceries is that their size can accommodate a much wider variety of foods. Let's take a look at some of the new trends that have emerged from this superstore culture.

Trend 1

Now we have the "ethnic food aisle" where you can find East Indian, Chinese, Caribbean, and other ethnic products, depending on the demographics of your neighborhood. Take a look at the list of foods in the international foods section that follows and see which of those items are available in your store.

Trend 2

There's the "healthy lifestyle"—or what I refer to as the Birkenstock aisle—where the organic cereals, granola bars, etc., are grouped as if for a special cult. Most of what you will find here is not gluten-free, but you might find a safe organic breakfast cereal, rice cakes, or some other treat.

Trend 3

With the sudden rise in awareness of food intolerance, the mass-market grocery stores are starting to cater to the likes of you and me. Now you can find rice milk and soy milk. However, you do need to check these for barley and malt. Lactose-free milk and yogurt as well as tofu and rice cheese substitutes can all be found in the dairy cases. Rice crackers and rice cakes have become mainstream and on more than one occasion I have even found rice bread in the freezer! A wide selection of rice noodles—the Asian types as well as a variety of Italian rice and corn pastas—are now available in every shape from penne to fettuccini.

Trend 4

Some stores have a diabetic shelf and a *gluten-free shelf*! If this keeps up I may not have to visit a health food store anymore! What's even nicer about this new abundance of gluten-free options is that when friends want to feed me, they can access non-poisonous foods as readily as those they might normally purchase. It's also wonderful to have these products become more mainstream, as it cuts down on the suspicious looks my meals have been known to receive from less worldly gluten-ivores.

Although I'm encouraging you to get out there and try new foods, you must remember to scrutinize each new product that enters your mouth. This will involve a lot of reading, and I'll bet you'll even broaden your vocabulary. You'll have to learn more about what those scary words with too many consonants really mean. In other words, there's more than one way to spell gluten! Keep the forbidden ingredient list in your wallet until you become familiar with ingredient names. Once you get into the swing of things, you'll be jostling for position in the checkout line as quickly as you used to.

Advocating Change

If your neighborhood store *isn't* making your shopping convenient, perhaps you should let them know how happy you'll be to spend your money at their establishment only when they start carrying the foods you need. Many stores have a suggestion board. If yours doesn't, ask to speak to the manager. They usually appreciate the feedback. After all, they do want your business. If there's a market for more cookies or waffles, chances are good that they *will* investigate and bring in more variety. If your neighborhood store can't support your requirements, try this approach at the health food shops.

Many health food stores can also provide you with lists of gluten-free products and suppliers who market to the gluten-free population. You might also want to promote your cause by leaving information with merchants. Letting them know that there's a swarm of potential customers out there may motivate them a little more to search out new gluten-free products.

Your local support group should also be able to provide you with a list of local "free" suppliers. If you're still unsatisfied with the variety of goods available in your neck of the woods, you should definitely check out the shopping sites on the Internet where the lists of gluten-free specialties you can spend your money on are endless.

The Dirty Dozen

On my last visit to Vancouver, a friend took me to a bakery where she said they made amazing rice-flour bread. I entered the store, glanced over the cases, and asked about the bread. The woman behind the counter showed me four different loaves. Then she proudly informed me that everything in the store was gluten-free. I was in shock. I took a step back from the glass counter display to take another look. My mouth dropped open. I checked that I had heard her correctly. I looked again at the beautiful display of delicacies, and I started to cry. I'm not kidding. I wept. You would have thought I had just won 10 million dollars. I was 30 years old and had never eaten focaccia, chicken pot pie, apple strudel, cinnamon buns…I didn't know where to start.

For the first time, I ate a grilled sandwich in a public space. It tasted so good that after my first bite I actually put it down in disbelief. This must be bad, I told myself. I can't eat this! It's a trick! I didn't eat much while I was in the bakery because I was sure it would make me sick. I did, however, take two bags of food back to my hotel. After a few hours had passed, I ate about three meals worth of baked goods. The next day, I took a long and expensive cab ride back for lunch, and got a few more bags of treasure to bring back on the plane. This fabulous bakery is called Panne Rizo and can be found listed in chapter 4.

Just down the street from my house, I've found a baker who sees flour as a cheap ingredient, and prefers to bake with things like ground nuts. She doesn't make everything gluten-free, but she does bake three incredible cakes that don't have any gluten. My family now often asks me to supply one of these cakes for events. This isn't only so that I can participate, it's because they're some of the best cakes any of them have ever eaten.

By nature, conventional bakeries are dangerous turf. They're full of gluten, and therefore, chances are that anything you come in contact with has also come in contact with the dirty white stuff. It's in the air. It's on the floor and the walls. It dusts the pans of most things concocted in there. If you're supersensitive you should stay a block away. If you're daring (or crazy) and want to attempt a special relationship with your local bakery, make sure that they're clear on all of the facts. You want them to be willing to take the time and effort to ensure that contamination is considered in all aspects of the baking process. This is a big responsibility. If you find an establishment that's up for the challenge, help create demand by sharing the information with your local Celiac Association chapter.

Some bakeries will do "gluten-free baking days," which are on or after the day that they scrub out the bakery, making cross-contamination less likely. The safest places, of course are the *gluten-free zone* bakeries. These businesses take their gluten-free status very seriously, and will usually verify that the mills and distributors from which they source their ingredients are also safe. The second-best bakery is one that markets to people with food intolerance. Generally speaking, they are conscientious about ingredients and will be careful that gluten-free means just that.

If we want to be catered to, we need to let bakers know there's a market. The more we make our requests known, the faster we're going to see "free" bakeries popping up in all of our cities, and the sooner we'll be fearlessly popping fresh-baked delicacies into our mouths.

Manufacturers

It's important to remain empowered. The support groups are out there to offer support. The job of taking care of you is yours. Don't be shy. Pick up the phone and ask questions. Call customer service departments and get the dirt on any possible gluten contamination. If you're comfortable with the phone conversation, hang up and hit the grocery store.

You can also write letters. Many support groups research the product offerings of companies. Letters are sent to the manufacturer informing them about the celiac condition, and the company in question is requested to provide lists of products that do and don't meet our criteria. If you have a product line that you'd like to know more about, contact your association.

An association is likely to get a faster response to such a request, as the company knows that the information will reach more potential customers. This doesn't mean that you can't find out more on your own. The following is a form letter that you can use or modify to suit your needs.

Dear _____,

I would like to learn more about your product line and wish to know which of your products are safe for people with celiac disease.

Celiac disease is a medical condition in which the absorptive surface of the small intestine is damaged by gluten, which results in the body's inability to absorb essential nutrients from foods. The only treatment for celiac disease is a gluten-free diet for life.

I would like to know if you can provide me with a current gluten-free product list so that I will know what I can safely purchase and consume.

The foods must exclude wheat, rye, barley, triticale, and oats and any products derived from these grains. It is essential that there be no trace of these grains introduced during production, storage, or packaging of your food.

It would also be helpful if hidden sources of gluten in the ingredients could be identified, such as wheat starch in spice and seasoning blends, the

---

---

source of natural flavoring (e.g., malt), wheat in hydrolyzed vegetable or plant protein, and sources of starch or modified food starch. I realize that it is not required by law to list all ingredients used in the packaging process. However, even very small amounts of gluten can be deleterious to people with celiac disease.

Thank you in advance for your time and efforts. If you have any questions, please contact me.

Sincerely,

_____

---

*This letter is adapted from a letter written by the Food Research Committee at the National Celiac Conference in Hamilton, Canada: May 26, 2000.

We also need to let companies know that they're losing customers by filling foods with unnecessary gluten. If a manufacturer has just changed product ingredients to include gluten, share your disappointment and the disappointment of at least one in 300 potential customers. We can complain all we want, but if we don't speak up to the people who can make a difference, our bellyaching will be just that. It's up to us to ensure that the producers of food consider the liability of adding gluten-containing ingredients to their recipes. Speak up, and you'll see more packages marked "gluten-free" on the shelves of the future.

Gluten-Free Around the World

In the meantime, we can find exotic foods from other parts of the world to satisfy our cravings. It's a big place, and we should never assume that we've seen and tried it all.

A couple of summers ago I was intent on getting my hands on some colorful paper Chinese lanterns to hang in my living room. My search, however, seemed in vain as I soon learned that shopkeepers bring these lanterns out only for Chinese New Year in February. My boyfriend, who I suppose was tiring of pulling the car over every time I saw an Asian gift shop, started making his own inquiries.

We were led from our regular stomping grounds to a completely unfamiliar neighborhood. We were directed to a Chinese mall, a place specializing in products for the Asian market. It was an incredible discovery. In our search for out-of-season paper lanterns we uncovered much more valuable treasure.

I had done plenty of digging in my neighborhood Chinatown and assumed that I had unearthed pretty well all of the rice-based gems that the Orient had to offer. The packaging, which is so whimsical and colorful, is what led me into what I almost want to call a Chinese candy store. There were all kinds of jars in the center of the shop filled with pickled, dried, sugared, and salted roots, fruits, and bits that I couldn't recognize. All along the walls were shelves full of plastic packages containing cookies, crackers, and various snack foods.

This store, like the rest of the mall, was clearly catering to those who read and spoke Chinese, so there was no English signage. On some items there was a picture of what was inside the bag or box. On some you could see through the clear package. On others you had to take a guess based purely on the ingredients. Most of the items had a white typed label of the ingredients in English stuck on the package. I could tell by reading the ingredients whether or not the product was gluten-free. What I couldn't tell was whether or not they would be palatable to me.

"Digging into boring pie. Getting out of boring time" was the only English I found on the side of a bag that I assumed contained crackers. Their marketing line was more likely to frighten me than entice, but I bought them none the less. I've never tasted anything in my life that I could compare them to. These thick, round, sweet, and spicy rice crackers turned out to be so tasty that I had to hide them from the boyfriend.

We came away from that mall with not only too many paper lanterns, but two grocery bags full of gluten-free goodies. This is my favorite kind of adventure. Instead of being the one who goes without, you'll be the person who introduces new and exotic foods to those who live in a less exciting world of white bread and pretzels. These people need some boring pie!

As a North American, I feel I have a lot to be grateful for, not the least of which is that I live in a very multicultural society. This means that I'm exposed to many different cultures and their diets. There are places on this planet where no one bats an eye if you don't eat wheat.

On my wanderings through ethnic neighborhoods and markets, I look for foods that are always made without gluten and wheat. I want to find new foods—not foods that are converted to meet our "special" needs. It can be pretty intimidating to walk into a store where all the packaging is in a language that you don't understand. Make a point of talking to the people who work in stores where you're not familiar with the food. You can also ask other customers questions about what certain foods are and how to prepare them. I've generally found that people are very happy to share their knowledge and experience with you. If the ingredients on ethnic food packaging have been translated and the translation seems a bit ambiguous, find out more before you take any chances. Contacting manufacturers can be a little more complicated if a product is made in Thailand, but not impossible. To find out more, contact the local distributor of the food item in question and have them investigate further for you. If you can't find a distributor's number marked on the product, ask the merchant.

The following is a small taste of what I've discovered in ethnic foods in the way of gluten-free carbohydrate or starch foods.

Chinese

Chinese grocery stores often carry many foods from other Asian countries, including Thailand, Vietnam, and Japan. Look for the following East Asian items:

Rice paper disks

These round, semi-transparent disks come in two sizes. When soaked in warm salted water, they soften and go white. They're used to make cold Thai spring rolls, which are chewy on the outside, filled with crunchy vegetables, and served with a spicy dip. The larger disks can also be used as a sandwich wrap. Look for spring roll inspiration in the recipe chapter.

Dried rice noodles

Rice noodles come in many widths and thicknesses. Boil them in salted water until they're soft, and use for pasta or stir-fry dishes.

Rice vermicelli

These are the thinnest of the rice noodles. They're very fine and should not be boiled, but soaked in very hot salted water until softened.

Fresh rice noodles

These are more substantial than the dried variety and need to be refrigerated. Stir the thicker noodles in oil before warming so they don't clump together. But before you use them, do check the ingredients, as another form of starch is sometimes added.

Bean thread

These clear and slightly chewy noodles are the same width as the rice vermicelli, but are made out of green beans. Soak them in boiled salt water until they're soft and add them to stir fries and broth soups.

Glutinous or sweet rice

This rice is usually used for making Asian desserts. Try it in rice pudding recipes.

Rice crackers

You'll be blown away by the variety of shapes and textures available in Chinese specialty food stores. In one shop I bought four types of rice crackers, all completely different. While the variety of flavors is appealing, watch the seasonings, and avoid any with questionable soy sauce in the flavoring. Not very environmentally friendly, many come in individually wrapped packages—making them convenient for lunches.

Tapioca crackers with black sesame

These look a lot like the rice papers you use to make spring rolls, only instead of soaking them in water, you slip them into a very hot oven for a few seconds, and they expand to crunchy and slightly gritty crackers. Broken into shards, they're very impressive in a bowl at a party or potluck. Serve them with your favorite dips.

Prawn crackers

When deep-fried, these swell up into delicious light and crunchy chips, which are served with peanut sauce. These are very popular in Thai restaurants and are sometimes called shrimp chips. They're inexpensive and easy and fast to make (you can make them in seconds) and they're real crowd pleasers.

Sesame cookies

Sesame cookies are nothing like conventional cookies. These large, flat, soft, and chewy disks are made of sesame, peanuts, and sugar. If you like peanut buttery things, you'll love these. Think fruit leather. Rip them into pieces and eat them as they are, or cut them into strips and wrap them around other things—like carrot sticks for after-school snacks.

Almond cakes

Almond cakes are hard and more like cookies. They're made with bean flour, almond powder, and lots of sugar, making them very sweet and somewhat grainy in texture. They usually come in a box. Splurge for the more expensive brands and enjoy them with a cup of tea.

Snack foods

Not unlike our potato chip aisle, Chinese markets offer all kinds of things to munch on. Many of them are made from rice, corn, or tapioca. But again, you'll have to watch out for soy seasoning. You're in for a surprise because it's hard to tell whether they're sweet, savory, or spicy by what you see on the packaging. Doesn't really matter—they're all yummy.

Bean curd jellies

Perhaps the name of these snacks could be a little more appealing, but it doesn't keep the kids from loving them. These little cups of gelatin come in all kinds of fruit flavors from grape to lychee, and they're terrific for packing in lunches.

Bean paste rice cakes

I'm sure the name of these in Chinese is much more appetizing. These very sweet and slightly gritty little layer cakes are made with rice flour. I've cut them into little squares and served them to friends with tea. They cleared the plate.

Flours

You can find white rice flour as well as "sweet" or "glutinous," which is not gluten, but indicates that it has a stickier consistency because it's made from sticky rice. The glutinous rice flour is used in making traditional Chinese desserts. Potato starch as well as tapioca flour and the grains used to make tapioca pudding can also be found in Asian food markets.

Indian

Indian grocery stores are full of "free" options. This is another culture where rice is a staple, but bean flours are also used in a wonderful variety of ways. Again, *always* read the ingredients. Cheaper brands may break convention and add gluten as fillers.

Basmati rice

Basmati rice is an aromatic long grain rice that's also popular in Middle Eastern countries, but it's widely agreed that the best basmati comes from India.

Papadum

Papadum are round crackers made from lentil flour, baking soda, and spices. You put these under the grill, or deep-fry them until they expand into delicious crunchy flat "bread." Serve them as an accompaniment to a meal or as a snack. They come in lots of sizes and degrees of spiciness.

Snacks

Packaged like bags of chips, most of these snacks are made from chickpea (*besan*) flour. Available in all kinds of shapes and textures, these highly addictive nibbles are a great hit at parties or as bar snacks. Watch out for the very spicy ones!

Cassava chips

Just like potato chips, these are made from the cassava root. You can find them salted or seriously spiced.

Dosa mixes

Dosas are thin crepe-like savory pancakes made from rice and lentil flour. Fill them with curried potatoes or anything you like and fold them in half like an omelet. These take some practice. Traditionally cooked on a "*tava*," they can also be made in a heavy skillet. Try them in a restaurant the first time, so you know what to expect.

Idli mixes

The box reads "rice lentil cake mix," but these are traditionally served as an appetizer or bread. Idli molds are used to create the perfectly round, savory little steamed cakes. You can also pour the mixture into small ramekin dishes and steam them in an inch or so of water in a large saucepan. Fry the batter in a hot, dry pan to make little fluffy pancakes. Another one you might want to try in a restaurant before trying at home.

Mumra

You can find rice that is puffed and hollow like breakfast cereal. It's not toasted however, so it's very white. Toast it quickly in the oven and it will turn golden, crispy, and perfect for making rice crispy treats.

Rice sooji

Not to be confused with *sooji* (or *sujee*), which is wheat. This crushed rice can be cooked up into a hot rice cereal, like the expensive version you find in health food stores. Serve it as you would porridge with brown sugar, cinnamon, and raisins.

Desserts!

If you can find a place that makes traditional Indian desserts, you're in for a treat. Many are made from reduced milk or chickpea flour and ground almonds, cashews, or pistachios. The main flavorings are saffron and cardamom, and in many cases the only difference between the sweets is the texture, which is changed because of the temperatures at which they're cooked. Look for:

- *Ladoo:* These little fried balls are like sugary donut centers but they're made from chickpea flour and caramelized sugar. This is the only deep-fried sweet on the list. If you find these, ensure that wheat-laden treats were not fried in the same oil.
- *Mohanthal:* Made of the same ingredients as the ladoo, mohanthal is baked rather than deep fried.
- *Barfi:* This very milky tasting sweet has the texture of fudge. Made mainly of milk, barfi (or burfi) comes in flavors like chocolate and pistachio.
- *Penda:* Made of the same ingredients as barfi, penda is cooked at a different temperature and has more of a cheesecake texture. Again, look for an assortment of flavors from saffron to almond.
- *Pak:* Pak could be confused with barfi or penda as it has the qualities of both.
- *Badam mesub:* This hard cake is made from ground almonds and *ghee* (clarified butter). It has a flavor similar to shortbread and the texture of pralines.
- *Kaju katri:* This candy is made from ground cashews, sugar, milk powder, and cardamom. Think exotic fudge.

Do speak to the vendors of these goods before taking my word on them. According to the place where I shop, the traditional recipes for these items are "free." Should you track these sweets down, I suggest you buy an assortment and cut them up into little squares. Skip lunch and invite some friends over.

Indian markets also offer an incredible array of flours available for cooking and baking:

- *Besan* or *gram*: chickpea flour
- *Urid*: white lentil flour (black lentils with skins removed)
- Green and yellow *moong* (mung) bean flour
- Yellow split pea flour
- *Bajri*: millet flour
- *Juvar* (*juar*): sorghum flour

Most packaging in Indian food stores is in English, but they do use a couple of other words mixed in, which spell gluten. Be sure to watch out for these four when reading ingredients:

- *Maida*
- *Sujee* or *Sooji*
- *Chapatti* flour
- *Rava*

These all translate into wheat or semolina. When verifying with shop owners, let them know that you need to avoid these ingredients as well.

Japanese

Unfortunately, much of what you will find in Japanese specialty shops is highly processed—so read very carefully. There are some fantastic simpler foods to look for, such as:

Mochi

Mochi is pronounced "mo-chee." It can be organic (health food stores often carry a brown rice version) or highly processed. This rice cake goes into the oven as a hard block and comes out doughy and chewy. Made with sticky rice, this versatile food item is served sweet as a dessert rolled in sugar (you'll find it ready to eat with bean paste centers), or savory rolled in a soy powder and spices. It can also be toasted, cut up, and tossed into soups to make a kind of rice dumpling.

Miso

Miso is a savory and salty paste made from fermented soy, rice, and salt. This is used to make sauces and miso soup. You must beware that sometimes barley or wheat is used in the fermentation process, and this is not always easy to find out. Not unlike with soy in Chinese cuisine, you must verify that it is "free."

Yam noodles

These noodles are often sold in little bundles that look like tiny bird nests. They're already cooked and only need be dropped into hot broth to be reheated. Think of them as rice noodle dumplings.

Fried soy bean curd

These cakes of tofu look like they've been battered, but they're pure tofu with a lovely texture. Simply cut up the little blocks and add to stir-fried vegetables. This is the form of tofu you'll find in Pad Thai as well.

Rice

Look for short grained Japanese rice that's especially made for making sushi and "sticky rice." Cooked in less water than you would use for other varieties (1 to 1), it clumps together, making it easy to eat with chopsticks. For instructions, see chapter 8.

Ginger, red bean, or green tea ice cream

If you like ice cream, you definitely won't be disappointed by these exotic flavors.

Latin

In Latin America, rice is an important part of the diet, but corn is also used extensively.

Soft white corn tortillas

These are like flat bread. You can warm them on a griddle or in the microwave. Hearty corn tortillas are a staple in many South American and Mexican dishes. You can also use soft tortillas as sandwich wraps. Read carefully, and don't confuse them with the soft wheat flour version.

Yellow corn tortillas

These crunchy, thinner tortillas are made with cornmeal rather than corn flour. They're like the Americanized taco, except flat. You warm them up on a griddle or in the oven and use them as a base for refried beans and cheese and eat them like a crispy pizza. In restaurants this is called a tostada. You can also break them up as chips and serve them with soup or bean stews. Use your imagination!

Flan

Flan is a kind of firm custard or pudding that you can buy as a mix or ready-made in a tin. Made from milk, it has a sweet and delicate flavor.

Instant polenta

Now you can make polenta in five instead of 25 minutes. It's basically treated cornmeal in a bag. It's not the most economical format to buy cornmeal in, unless time is more valuable to you than money.

Masa harina

Masa or *maizena* is white corn flour that's milled to a very fine consistency and is used for making tortillas and for baking.

Plantain chips

This snack food is made from fried plantain. Although they look a lot like banana chips, these crispy chips are savory rather than sweet. Also look for these in stores specializing in foods from tropical climates.

Italian

Ready made polenta rolls

This polenta only needs to be unwrapped and warmed up. You can grill it or fry it and serve it with sauce or pizza toppings. It's now available plain or flavored with herbs and sun-dried tomatoes. Perfect for no-fuss instant dinners.

Instant polenta

This is the same kind as you get in South American shops to be used for that five-minute polenta dinner.

Arborio rice

This short grain starchy rice is the most common form of Italian rice that you can buy for making risotto. It's usually available in regular grocery stores as well. My friend and I've decided that there's a "risotto conspiracy" that has people believing this is a dish for experienced chefs only. This very satisfying concoction is exposed in chapter 8 as the easy-to-make dinner it really is.

Carnaroli rice

This is similar to arborio rice but has even more starch. More starch means a creamier risotto.

Riso Vialone

Riso Vialone is the highest quality risotto rice available. It has the smallest grains and the most starch.

Pasta secca

Italian bakeries make a lot of interesting confectionery with almonds, sugar, and egg whites. Be sure to find out about floured baking sheets and other possible contamination concerns. If you can find a bakery you trust, buy a big pastry box full of these marzipan-like cookies.

Middle Eastern

There are many countries and cultures in the Middle East, but I find that a lot of the diets overlap one another. Look for the following foods in Arab, Lebanese, Greek, or Persian food shops:

Falafel mixes

When you order falafel in a restaurant, it's often made with wheat. The mixes you find in the stores, however, are often made only of ground, dried beans and spices. These are a great source of protein and super easy to make. I use very little oil rather than deep frying, and they turn out just great!

Flours

Middle Eastern cultures also use rice flour and chickpea flour.

Halvah

Halvah is an interesting gritty candy made of ground almonds, ground sesame, or ground peanuts mixed with sugar and honey. Almond is considered the best, but I like any form I can get my hands on! Sometimes it comes in slabs wrapped in cellophane, but it's also sold in plastic tubs. Arabs eat a softer version of halva that they spread on bread. This isn't a health food, but because I like to eat so much of it, I try to focus on the fact that it's high in protein and calcium.

Rice flour cookies

Persian shops sell rice flour butter cookies with poppy seeds on top and small clover-shaped cookies made from chickpea flour. These are often enjoyed only on special occasions. The traditional recipes for these cookies contain no flour. This doesn't mean anything, however. Try to buy them from the bakery, rather than the shop that sells them amongst other things. I've bought them only to find that the bottoms were coated with flour from the baking trays.

Kosher

Make a note of checking the kosher section of your grocery store around Passover (early spring). Food that's clearly labeled "Kosher for Passover" cannot be made with wheat. To confuse things, it *can* be made with *matzo* (which is wheat). If an item doesn't contain *matzo*, it's gluten-free. Many products (like cookies and treats) that are made with no wheat whatsoever are only available during this period. Hasidic Jews don't eat products made with *matzo* during Passover. If you have an Hasidic neighborhood near you, it might be well worth your wheat-free efforts to investigate! Look for products like potato pancake mixes and chocolate macaroon cookies.

There's a whole gluten-free world out there—and I've only just scratched the surface of it. I encourage you to do your own exploring. Next time you're approaching an ethnic shop, don't walk on by—step in. If you're not sure where these shops exist in your city, why not check out the Yellow Pages? You can also check in the White Pages for groups like cultural societies. Call them and ask about places to buy their specialties. When you visit cosmopolitan cities, be sure to search out the bigger stores for even more variety. I'll bet you'll be throwing some very interesting dinner parties!

And with this world of possibilities, how can you go wrong? I hope this chapter has inspired you to hop on the subway or plan a shopping road trip. But before you put on your coat, take a look some last essentials...

7

THE MEALS

Enough on Your Plate

All people are made alike.
They are made of bones, flesh and dinners.
Only the dinners are different.

—Gertrude Louise Cheney

Outside of the Box

Today, everyone is autonomous. A six-year-old can pull dinner from the freezer, place it in the microwave, and serve it in seven minutes. This dinner is individually packaged and eaten, which means that "dinnertime" is less of an event. For many families, communication comes in the form of a note left on the counter beside the frozen or canned foodstuff to be heated up.

We've all heard about how in the Mediterranean, people eat huge meals, drink lots of wine, and don't suffer from the heart disease that North Americans do. This has been attributed to a couple of important factors. Everyone is expected to show up when the family sits down together because the meal is sacred. Food is celebrated. Food is fresh, seasonal, and homemade.

You don't need to be home all day cooking like an old-style Italian mama to bring that continental feel to your meal times. With a little foresight, you can whip up a fabulous dinner in less than 20 minutes. How inconvenient is this? Will you really miss spending five times more for individual freezer-burnt portions soaked in questionable preservatives, additives, sodium, and gluten? That extra 13 minutes could add considerably to your lifespan.

What's happened to our lives that sustenance is had in energy bar form twice a day, and a frozen dinner is eaten at night? If you've read the ingredients on the side of that frozen dinner, you'll realize that you're not robbing your family of anything by depriving them of instant meals. Today's boil-in-the-bag and microwave dinners look like they were designed for the starship Enterprise. We're light years away from producing processed foods that have nutritional value.

Simple foods are easier for our bodies to digest, and the simpler the food is, the more likely you are to actually taste the essence of what you're eating. Today's foods are so refined and processed that they require additives and complicated sauces to make them palatable. More complicated means more gluten. Starting with small steps like the condiments you choose, you can begin to make your diet healthier since you'll be running into less gluten.

Some Natural and Naturally "Free" Condiments

- Olive oil, sunflower, canola, flaxseed, peanut, and sesame oils (verify that they are 100% *pure*)
- Lemon or lime juice
- Balsamic vinegar, wine vinegar, and apple cider vinegar
- Fresh herbs and ground spices
- Sea salt and fresh ground pepper
- Homemade or organic fruit preserves and jams
- Homemade or organic herb infused oils
- Ground nut butters from almonds or sunflower seeds
- Tahini (sesame seed paste)

These basics can be found in any market. You'll cut back on chemicals and preservatives, and your whole family can enjoy their food prepared in the same way. Requesting that your food be prepared with these ingredients will also make it easier to eat safely in restaurants. Remember that food doesn't have to be labeled as such to be convenient. Simply being organized can make mealtime a hassle-"free" event. Have a plan, make a list, and shop for the meals you intend to make in any given week.

It's a good idea to keep food staples in the house so that you can always whip up something quickly. It's also wise to:

- Cook more than you need so leftovers can be integrated into other meals or frozen.
- Cook more of the plain grains, rice, or potatoes that can become pilafs, pancakes, and casseroles in future meals.
- Create one-pot meals like stews, chili, risotto, or lasagna.
- Ask for help with prep work and clean up.
- Take turns making the meals.

At home, play some inspiring or relaxing music in your kitchen. Why not pour yourself a glass of wine? Talk to your kids, partner, or a friend about the day's events while you heat up some soup and warm cornbread in the oven before everyone runs off to their evening events.

Food isn't complicated, but commerce has made it that way. Food is gorgeous, satisfying, and pleasurable just the way nature made it. We don't have to do much to make a meal enjoyable. So, set the table and gather around it with the people you love. Pass the spuds and share some stories. *That* is what meals are all about.

Up for the Challenge

Many of us eat breakfast standing over the kitchen sink like zombies, shoveling in whatever instant form of carbohydrate we can find. Unless you're a morning person, you may be one of the many who neglect breakfast in the name of "just a few more minutes" of sleep. Thank goodness there are lots of no-fuss "free" options to wake our comatose taste buds.

Everything that exists in a gluten world has been replicated into a healthier format, including bread, waffles, cereals (both hot and cold), and muffins. I eat these for breakfast on most days, but I always try to add protein to the equation. Eating straight carbohydrates will cause insulin levels to rise quickly. This means that in a very short time, your sugar levels will crash and you'll be craving more carbs. Adding protein (even if it's only peanut butter) to your meal helps to slow the rate of insulin volatility. An even better approach is to soft-boil or scramble an egg or some tofu.

If a bowl of cereal is as extreme as you can go, why not keep a jar of raisins and walnuts or toasted almonds beside the cereal box and sprinkle them on top for a more exciting and nutritionally complete start? Use "free" soy milk instead of regular. You can do this in your sleep. Or take a look at the following lists of "free" foods, which are organized according to how long they take to prepare.

Some More Leisurely Options

1. Frittatas made with fresh vegetables, grated Parmesan, and sundried tomatoes
2. Rice or chickpea pancakes piled up with maple syrup and sliced bananas or berries
3. Latkes fried crispy and served with applesauce or sour cream
4. French rice toast drenched in maple syrup
5. Omelets folded over Brie or avocado and smoked salmon
6. Crispy bacon and eggs over easy with "free" toast soldiers
7. Fried or grilled polenta with scrambled eggs, chives, and some sliced tomato
8. Savory home fries made with last night's potatoes, some onions, and fennel seeds
9. Herbed "free" sausages served with warm grapes
10. Baked apples or stewed fruit—*au natural* or topped with "free" crumble
11. Bread pudding made with rice bread and plenty of cinnamon and vanilla

Fast Fixes

1. Toast with toasted almond or pistachio butter
2. "Free" cereal sprinkled with currants, dried cherries, and pecans
3. Whole grain "free" toaster-waffles with nut butter
4. Healthy rice pudding—enjoyed straight from the fridge or gently warmed
5. Fruit smoothies with yogurt or soy milk whipped up in the blender
6. Lightly scrambled or soft-boiled eggs (quick in a pot or the microwave)
7. Warm grain cereals like millet, quinoa, or rice with raisins, milk, and cinnamon

8. Reheated bean cakes or chickpea patties (see page 114)

9. Any yummy leftovers from last night's dinner

On the Run

1. Previously toasted almonds kept fresh in a jar—enjoy with dried apricots

2. Individual fruit cups or applesauce

3. Fruit, such as a banana or an apple, that travels well

4. "Free" muffins or banana bread that doesn't need fussing

5. Yogurt—now available lactose-free, too (toss in some raisins and nuts!)

Oatmeal has long been a traditional breakfast on very cold winter mornings. There's been much discussion lately about whether or not oats are friendly, which is due to the possibility of contamination during the milling process. When I was little, my mother used to make me rice baby food cereal for breakfast instead of the oatmeal she made my brother. I loved the flavor, and was still eating it on winter mornings at the ripe old age of 12. I remember having to threaten my little brother that he'd be flattened if word of my breakfast habits were leaked at school.

You might not be ready for this, but recently I've gotten into cold leftover brown rice with plain or vanilla soy milk and a bit of brown sugar (like cold porridge). I can't believe how good the flavor and texture are! If I owned a microwave, I might try this with warmed leftover brown rice. I guess it's just a lazy girl's rice pudding. (Give this a try with leftover millet or buckwheat, too!) Whatever you do, it's important to embrace variety in your diet to escape boredom and to ensure that you're getting enough nutrition. If you're concerned about your vitamin intake, it might make sense to take a multivitamin supplement. Most will indicate whether or not they're "free" on the label.

Breakfast is a meal for which you'll have to be prepared. Every coffee shop is full of donuts and croissants. You won't find a power bar or breakfast bar on the market that's friendly, so try to avoid looking to your local convenience store for morning sustenance. Remember that what you choose to put in your mouth to start the day is very important, like good fuel in a car. On the bright side, you'll be running on healthier fuel than you're probably used to. Before you know it, you'll be up at 5 am for a jog. Okay, maybe you'll just start the day in a better mood.

The Brown Bag

I remember how as a child, what your lunch pail looked like said a lot about you. My first one was blue, and sported a Holly Hobby decal. My second had a Barbie motif. As I matured, it became more and more important that I show up for school with the standard-issue brown paper bag. In a perfect world, mothers bought them in bulk in a plastic wrapper, indicating that their purpose was for carting the lunches of the socially acceptable child. Nowadays, I don't think that children of our environmentally responsible age would relate to the angst that a child of the '70s felt when her mother packed her lunch in the reused milk bag instead.

We've been brainwashed as to what a lunch is supposed to look like. Take a look at those sandwich bags, which tuck away a slice of Wonder Bread like a glove. Every child in North America knows that lunch is supposed to consist of a peanut butter and jelly sandwich on white bread. Even crusts are optional.

I could just cry thinking about those sandwiches of my childhood. I used to keep them suffocated in plastic wrap so that they wouldn't fall apart as I bit into them. I don't think I've packed a sandwich in 15 years. If you're ready to move beyond the limitations of that 5 x 5 plastic baggie, you'll have to take a few things into consideration when planning a less conventional lunch. For example:

- Can it be eaten cold, or does it need to be nuked?
- Does it need to be refrigerated, or will it survive a few hours in a knapsack?
- Will it require utensils, or can it be eaten with your hands?

You might want to consider whether the food you pack could be embarrassing to eat in front of others. This is a particularly important question when dealing with children. If the lunch you provide attracts a lot of unwanted attention in the lunchroom, your child will be less likely to eat it. He or she might go hungry, or worse, might eat something from someone else's lunch pail. It's also important to take into consideration how manageable the lunch is:

- Will you be somewhere you can you prepare it just before you eat it?
- Does it require pre-assembly?
- Can it survive being assembled the night before?

If you don't have access to a microwave where you eat your lunch, invest in a good thermos. This does require that you heat something up in the morning, but it will offer you a lot more options than one of those sandwich bags can.

It's also a good idea to invest in some good quality plastic containers (e.g., Tupperware). The dollar store kind is not usually good for the long haul—you're going to want them to be both dishwasher and microwave safe.

Plan dinners that make good leftovers and cook larger quantities. Lasagna, for example, can be separated and placed in the fridge right after dinner so that it's ready the next morning. Soups and sauces also freeze well and can be pulled out of the freezer the night before. Same thing with baked goods. Individually wrap cake portions and muffins, freeze them and pull them out as you need them. When stocking up the freezer, you can rotate leftovers so that they don't seem repetitive. Remember that a little bit of planning ahead can save you time and grief in the morning. Here are some "free" ideas for lunches:

Hot Lunch Options

The following options will require that you either have a microwave, kettle, or can opener on hand—or a thermos.

Soup

Soup alone is a satisfying lunch, but it can also be enjoyed with accompaniments. You can pack homemade soup in a container and heat it in the microwave if you have one available where you dine, or warm it in the morning and bring it with you in a thermos. Should you have the facilities, you can also have canned soups or one of the "free" organic instant soups where you only have to add hot water. Keep them stored in your desk or locker for the days when you're too rushed, and for emergencies. Enjoy soup with rice crackers, nacho chips, or dry toast. You can toast a bunch of bread and pack it in an airtight container, where it will keep for days.

Beans

Beans are high in protein and very filling, making them a terrific lunch option. A can of baked beans can either be warmed on site or taken in a thermos. Instant chili is available in cups and only requires hot water. Both are wonderful with nacho chips or with…

Soft corn tortillas

Corn tortillas are best when warmed. Enjoy them as flat bread, ripping off pieces and dipping them into your soup or chili, or use them as a "wrap" sandwich.

Leftovers

No one wants to think they're eating leftovers, but some foods seem to taste better the second time around. Take a look at some of these leftover food ideas, which we'll get into further in chapter 8. The following are a good option because they travel and reheat well, and taste just as delicious the second and third time around:

- Potato pancakes
- Pakora
- Falafel
- Pizza
- Lasagna
- Cabbage rolls
- Frittatas and omelets
- Baked potatoes
- Risotto or rice pilaf
- Polenta
- Pasta

Cold Lunch Options

The following are a few of many options that can be enjoyed any time and any place.

- Nacho chips with salsa
- Sushi and California rolls
- Hard-boiled eggs or devilled eggs
- Dolmates
- Avocados to spread on things
- "Free" cold cuts
- Cans of tuna or salmon (don't forget to pack a can opener)
- Rice crackers with cheese or pâté
- Dips with veggies like carrots, red peppers, and cucumber slices
- Leaf salad (put dressing in a little container so it doesn't go soggy)
- Bean salad, lentil salad, or chickpea salad
- Potato salad

- "Free" pasta salad
- Tuna salad or egg salad served on a bed of greens
- Rice salad
- Fruit
- Did I mention rice cakes?
- "Free" cookies, cake, or cupcakes
- "Free" muffins or banana bread
- Little packs of puddings, fruit cups, or apple sauce
- Rice pudding
- Yogurt or lactose-free yogurt
- Trail mix, raisins, nuts, and dried fruit
- Cheese or tofu cheese
- Leftovers that you don't mind eating cold (e.g., pizza, chicken drum sticks, grilled chicken breast)

Especially for the Kiddies

When preparing food for kids, the trick is to keep things interesting *and* kid-friendly. Ask your child what his or her classmates get in their lunches so that she or he will feel involved in preparing and choosing lunches wherever possible. This will help to ensure that the lunch gets eaten. Here are a few ideas to start with:

- "Free" macaroni and cheese packed in a thermos
- Baked beans or soup
- Nacho chips with mild salsa
- Hot dogs without fillers (can be heated, then eaten cold)
- Jello with diced fruit
- Celery or carrots with peanut butter
- Popcorn
- Rolled up ham and other "free" cold cuts
- Cheese or tofu cheese slices
- Little packs of puddings, fruit cups, apple sauce
- Yogurt or lactose-free yogurt
- Grapes, bananas, apples, and oranges
- Rice crackers with cheese or peanut butter
- Flavored rice cakes
- "Free" cookies and cupcakes
- "Free" banana bread
- Nuts and raisins

- "Free" cereal in a baggie (can be eaten as a snack)
- Candy treats or bags of chips on special days
- Fruit juice drink boxes (you can freeze these to keep lunches cool)
- Rice and soy milk in individual box format (if your child is lactose intolerant)

Make shopping lists with lunches in mind before you hit the grocery store, and whenever possible, make lunches the night before. Your lunches are only going to get better (and probably healthier) as a result of the new diet, since you won't be jamming something between two slices and calling it a meal anymore. Now, just imagine what's going to happen to *dinners*!

No Matter How You Slice It

Gluten-free bread has come a very long way from its humble (or should I say crumble?) beginnings. Nowadays, with the growing market, there are many varieties available made with combinations of rice, potato, corn, tapioca, and so on. Yet despite the variety available today, many bakeries still haven't figured out how to produce bread that doesn't slice into crumbly dry slabs.

Depending on where you live, you may be enjoying some terrific bread. I'll never forget that bakery in Vancouver where I couldn't finish my sandwich because the bread was so good and I was afraid that they'd tricked me. In Toronto, where I live, we have half a dozen different local bakeries that offer "free" bread varieties, but many are still a bit disappointing. The demands of the growing "free" market have prompted my local health food store to start bringing in bread all the way from California. If you're not satisfied with the quality of the bread made available in your neighborhood, talk to your local merchants.

Keep in mind, too, that fresh bread doesn't have to be a painful memory. If you take a look at the front cover of Bette Hagman's new book, *The Gluten-Free Gourmet Bakes Bread*, you'll have a hard time believing that those sinful-looking loaves on the book jacket are in fact "free." Have a garage sale and sell your rarely used kitchen equipment; you can use the dough to buy a bread maker.

To this day, I won't even entertain the idea of eating most packaged rice bread unless it's made a trip to the toaster first. Slipping the bread impersonator into a toaster greatly improves its texture and strength, and gives the anemic little rectangles a healthier glow. With some of the bread, I've learned that open-face sandwiches are the best way to go. Less bread, less money, more flavor from the filling and less agitation for the roof of my mouth.

You can also keep your eyes open for bread made with bean flours, which are a healthy alternative because they're higher in protein, nutrients, and fiber. There are also better mixes available that use these flours for less crumbly and more satisfying bread. Check your local shelves and freezers. If your bread source could use a formula improvement, why not drop the manufacturer a line and find out what they know about bean flours?

Most gluten-free breads available at your local health food store are baked—well, locally. These bakeries are often small operations that deliver on a regular basis. To make sure that you're getting the freshest bread available, ask the store manager about what days the bakery delivers. It's also wise to stock up and keep a couple of extra loaves in the freezer for those weeks when you miss the shipment, or for over the holidays when the bakeries may not be delivering on their regular schedule.

Gluten-free bread doesn't have a long shelf life. Some of it can only be bought frozen, and those brands that aren't are often sold off the shelf only because it's expensive for stores to keep them in the fridge. The labels on the bread don't always tell you to refrigerate in order to stave off that ugly green hair. Always check baked goods carefully before purchasing, and don't buy anything that doesn't come with an expiry date. It can be very disappointing to bring home a five-dollar loaf of bread only to find the underside sprouting the aforementioned fuzz.

If you're freezing your bread and it doesn't come sliced, be sure to slice it up before you stash it in the freezer. Whether it came sliced or not, be sure to separate the slices by carefully jiggling them in the bag before you store them. Failing to do this will have you trying to chisel away your toast in the morning; it'll also warp your dinner knives.

If you're going to be toasting your bread, you might as well keep it in the freezer. On average, one loaf of gluten-free bread costs as much as four loaves of "regular" bread. And while we're talking economics, if the bread isn't sprouting hair yet but has been demoted to the reduced rack, try and snap it up at half price. If it's going into the freezer the same day, what difference does it make? The difference for me is that now I can justify another box of cookies!

Hail the Almighty Rice Cake

Once the terrain of leftover hippies in the 70s—and alien to the Wagon Wheel and Twinkie generation—the rice cake has finally achieved status as food for the masses. You may have grown to resent them, but I urge you to make peace with these Styrofoam disks, as they're a lot more than just emergency rations. First, let's take a look at the positive personality traits of our friend the rice cake:

- They're their own plate.
- They're cheap.
- They keep well, providing you seal the bag tight.
- They don't require refrigeration.
- They don't grow mold.
- They have no fat.
- They have little flavor. Yes, this is a benefit. Think of them as "carrier" food—they hold the toppings. (You don't imagine that processed white bread has much flavor either, do you?)
- They're lightweight. They may be bulky to pack when traveling, but they don't weigh anything. Once you eat them you free up a lot of space in your suitcase for souvenirs.
- They're always there when you need them. Why? Well, no one ever steals rice cakes.

Rice cakes are so mainstream now it's possible to find a huge variety of flavors—from chocolate chip to cheddar cheese. Some are even mixed with puffed corn, adding a whole new dimension of taste. However, beware of those that add gluten grains such as wheat germ. (Another sign that gluten-tolerant people consider them food.) And never assume that the sacred cakes are safe—always read the ingredients.

Now that we've established their stature—what should you do with them? As I mentioned above, the trick with rice cakes is to consider them a carrier food. Their mute flavor lends itself to being combined with both sweet and savory toppings.

The first consideration when working with these edible plates is to consider whether or not you want to assemble them well in advance, or put them together just before eating them. If, for example, you were carrying them in your purse to take with you on a day of errands, I'd avoid anything wet, as they'll go mushy within an hour of topping. With this in mind, I've split up some topping options based on convenience.

Toppings to Enjoy Right Away

(i.e., anything wet that is messy to prepare or could make the rice cake soggy)
- Tomato and pesto
- Avocado with salt and pepper
- Babaghanouj (roasted eggplant dip)
- Hummus (chickpea dip) or bean dip
- Sliced or mashed up banana
- Melted cheese. Try heating up rice cakes with cheese on them under the broiler. You can also melt cheese in the microwave; however, sometimes this can make the rice cakes a little chewy. Remember to watch them, since they tend to burn very quickly.
- Virtuous Rice Cake Pizza. You can also top them with tomato, pesto, green onions, and so on. Think of them as a very virtuous pizza!

To Enjoy Within a Couple of Hours

(i.e., anything with moisture that the rice cake will absorb if kept too long)
The trick to traveling with these is to stack them like you would two slices of bread to make a sandwich. Wrap tightly in cellophane if you have pieces of cheese or banana that could fall out, otherwise slip them into a sandwich bag.
- Cream cheese (you can add herbs and spices or buy flavored cheeses too)
- Cream cheese sprinkled with cinnamon and a little sugar
- Jams, jellies, and marmalade (also go great with cream cheese!)
- Medium and hard cheeses or tofu, soy, and rice "cheese"
- Chocolate hazelnut spread
- Peanut butter and sliced banana

The Go-All-Day Rice Cake:

I like to stack them up and carry them with me. The stickiness holds them together and the cakes stay super crunchy.
- Peanut butter
- Nut butters

For an alternative to peanut butter, try other kinds of nut butters like almond or hazelnut. Almost any kind of nut is available in butter form. If you can't find these locally, you can make them yourself in the food processor. The only ingredient is the nuts themselves, but you can add a little salt or canola oil if you like. You can also toast the nuts first to enhance the flavor. These homemade nut butters should be kept in the fridge for freshness.

One last rice cake trick is to eat them upside down when the topping permits. It sounds goofy, but if you eat them this way, you taste the topping more and the cake becomes pure crunch instead of a sponge to dry up your tongue.

If you can't get past your distaste for these passive little food impersonators, then keep some in the cupboard for emergency rations. There may be a moment in your life where you're relieved to have them come to your rescue.

Even if I can't talk you into rice cakes, I hope you've found inspiration in some of the many gluten-free options there are for meal times. I love a "fast-fix." In the next chapter, we'll explore some super-easy multicultural recipes that will add even more variety to your meals!

8
THE RECIPES

If You Can't Stand the Wheat, Get Into Your Kitchen

Arrowroot and Amaranth?

Baking would not rank as one of my favorite pastimes. However, there have been occasions where an overwhelming desire for a late night batch of peanut butter cookies has me beating a bowl of sugar and eggs with great fervor. And I tend to make a night of it, baking two or three batches of treats fueled by the concept of only one night of washing up. I go wild with the plastic wrap and stock up the freezer, as homemade baked goods have a shorter shelf life, and muffins, cornbread, or brownies all freeze pretty well. It's also harder to eat a whole batch of brownies in 24 hours if half of them are rock solid. (This has not, however, proven to be impossible; it's certainly helped me discover why we have back teeth!)

If you don't mind dishing out a few extra bucks, mixes can be a very convenient way to whip up a batch of chocolate brownies or rice bran muffins. You might want to keep a box in the cupboard for a quick fix. As a rule, it's a much better deal to bake from scratch, but if pre-mixed box baking is the route you want to go, then have no shame. You're not genetically built to *eat* baked goods; maybe you're not meant to *bake* them either. If you do want to have a go at it, read on.

I've mentioned that baking without gluten can be less forgiving than baking with wheat flour, but considering the following will increase your chances of success.

Tips for Converting "Regular" Recipes into "Free" Recipes

- Recipes that start with a smaller quantity of flour to begin with are likely to convert well.
- Recipes that use cake flour are good for converting because cake flour has less gluten in it than regular all-purpose flour, so your recipe is already less dependent on gluten.
- The more eggs in a recipe, the better they tend to convert. The thing to remember is that the properties of rice or soy flour are not the same as wheat flour. Gluten is the glue that is missing in gluten-free flour. Your recipe will be less crumbly if it has more binders in it to compensate for the lack of "glue."
- Buttering and flouring pans can be done just as well using rice flour.
- Using smaller pans or even better, a pan with a hole in the middle (like an angel food cake pan or a Bundt cake pan) helps cake batter to rise. For small pans, simply pour batter into two pans instead of one.
- When using stronger-flavoured flours (bean, soya, etc.), use spices like ginger, cinnamon, or sweet garam masala or a strong-flavoured ingredient like banana to mask flavour of flour.

On "Free" Baking in General

I can't say enough good things about Bette Hagman's cookbooks (see chapter 4), especially to those who already love to bake. Hagman is the pioneer in flour combining—and her books give you an opportunity to gain confidence before braving the gluten-free bakery front on your own. I blame a lot of pounds on Hagman. However, if you still want to take your own shot, get to know the following products.

Rice flour

Rice flour is a great substitute for wheat flour, but works best in combination with other flours.

Brown rice flour

Brown rice flour is almost as readily available as white. It can be a bit grittier and has a slightly nuttier taste, but is less refined and higher in fiber—meaning that it's better for you.

Gluten-free flour

There is an incredible selection of gluten-free flour available. Keep your eyes open in health food stores and ethnic markets for the following:

- Amaranth flour
- Arrowroot flour
- Bean flour (both dark and light)
- Brown rice flour
- Buckwheat flour (also known as kasha)
- Chestnut flour
- Chickpea flour (also known as garbanzo or besan)
- Corn flour, yellow
- Corn flour, white
- Cornmeal (also known as grits)
- Cornstarch
- Lentil flour
- Millet flour
- Moong bean flour
- Nut flours
- Pea flour
- Potato starch
- Potato flour
- Quinoa flour
- Sago flour
- Sorghum flour (also known as milo)
- Soy flour
- Sweet rice flour (also known as glutinous flour)
- Tapioca flour (also known as cassava or manoic)
- White rice flour

Xanthum and guar gum

Incorporate xanthum gum or guar gum into your baking recipes to give them more elasticity. You won't believe how they can improve a recipe that's normally crumbly. Ask for it in your health food store—it's usually found where the bulk spices are.

Baking powders

Baking powders consist of cream of tarter and baking soda, which are mixed with a starch ingredient—sometimes white flour. Make sure yours is wheat-free. It will be even better for you if it's free of aluminum too.

Fruits and veggies

Things like applesauce and bananas, zucchini, and carrots help muffins and cakes hold together better and stay moist longer.

Ground nuts

Look for baked-good recipes that utilize ground nuts instead of flour. They may be higher in fat, but they're also higher in protein and good for energy.

Make your own kits. Label jars in your refrigerator that contain pre-mixed dry ingredients for your favorite recipes. Take your flour combinations, baking powders or sodas, and spices, and mix them up well in enough quantity so that you can whip something together at a moment's notice. For example, I like to make chickpea-flour pancakes pretty regularly. I buy all of the necessary ingredients and combine enough to make them three or four times. Make up your mixes on a rainy Sunday afternoon, and next time you don't know what to make on a hectic weeknight, it won't be a big deal.

Keep a notebook for your baking experiments if you can't bring yourself to write in your cookbooks. And finally, remember that many gluten-free baked goods can be dry after a day or two—especially after freezing. A quick zap in the microwave can bring them back to life. If you don't have a microwave, cover in tin foil so that no moisture escapes and pop in a warm oven for a few minutes.

"Free" Cooking Tips

Cooking is a much more forgiving endeavor than baking. You don't need to learn a lot of tricks to successfully whip up "free" meals, just some common sense. Here are a few tips to help you through those times when gluten might want to rear its ugly head:

- Make your own "Shake and Bake" combinations for coating chicken and fish, and keep these labeled in jars in the refrigerator. This saves mixing up flours, crumbs, and spices when you're in a hurry. I find corn flour works particularly well, as does crushed "free" corn flake cereal.
- Use cornstarch to thicken sauces wherever flour is called for. Be careful with the quantities, though, as you'll need less cornstarch than you would flour. Start with a small amount, and add as required. It's also wise to mix the cornstarch with a little water in a cup first, instead of putting it directly into what you're thickening (this also helps to avoid lumps). A formula that works well is one teaspoon of cornstarch, tapioca, or potato starch to every tablespoon of wheat flour that a recipe calls for when used to thicken.
- Try cornmeal or a little cornstarch instead of breadcrumbs to hold hamburger meat together.
- Make pie shells for savory dishes using mashed potatoes, veggies, or nuts. If you want to convert a piecrust recipe for this sort of thing, then layer some grated cheese between the crust and the filling. It will help hold what might be a crumbly crust together while the fat in the cheese provides a water-resistant lining to help keep the crust from getting too soggy.
- Save breadcrumbs or bits of rice bread that have fallen apart in the freezer. These can be used whenever wheat breadcrumbs are used for filler. They don't work as well, however, when breadcrumbs are required to make something crispy. In that case, use cornmeal.

As you can see, this isn't rocket science. I only ever serve "free" versions of any dish to friends and family. And when I convert dishes that would traditionally call for gluten-containing ingredients, no one thinks my adaptation is inferior. So far, I've had nothing but compliments and requests for second helpings.

The Recipes

I enjoy spending time in the kitchen, but I'm also into instant gratification. If something is going to take more than two bowls or more than a few steps, I usually can't be bothered. I want to play.

The following is a collection of *ideas* for filling that space between the chicken breast and the broccoli on your plate—ideas for starch or carbohydrate foods. Please consider this an introduction only. I invite and encourage you to play with these recipes and make them your own. That said, instead of apologizing for deleting things from the dinner table, you'll soon find yourself enthusiastically introducing your discoveries to friends and family.

Rice

The types of rice we are most familiar with today hail from Asia. Rice is sold in its original form as "brown" rice, meaning that it still has its husk (the bran), or white, which means that its outer layer has been removed. There are many different varieties of brown and white rice available. There's long grain rice like basmati and jasmine, which has an exquisite aroma and works well for pilafs because the grains remain separated when cooked. Short grain rice, like Italian arborio and Asian sticky rice, have short, fat grains, which are very starchy and clump together or form a slightly more porridge-like consistency depending on how much liquid they're cooked in. Hundreds of other varieties fall between these two categories, and many of them are available at your local grocery store. For more exotic varieties of rice, visit your local health food store or gourmet food shop.

Cooking Long Grain Rice

For some people, cooking rice is quite intimidating. There are many techniques used around the world to cook rice. Of all of these, I find this method the simplest and most foolproof. This process steams the rice rather than boiling it, and it keeps the grains separated. You'll need:

    1 cup long grain rice, like basmati or jasmine
    1 1/2 cups water
    1/4 tsp salt

Rinse rice in a sieve under the tap until water runs clear.
Boil water with rice and salt in a heavy-bottom saucepan that has a tight fitting lid.
Cover when water is almost level with the rice and tiny holes appear in the surface of it.
Reduce heat to lowest temperature and let simmer for 10 min-

utes. Do not remove lid.

Remove from heat and let stand 5 more minutes. Keep covered.

Lift lid and fluff with fork.

Cooking Short Grain Sticky Rice

Use this method for cooking the short grain rice traditionally served in Oriental dishes. You'll need:

>   1 cup short grain rice, like Japanese sticky rice
>   1 cup water
>   1/4 tsp salt

Rinse rice in sieve until water runs clear.

Pour cold water, rice, and salt into saucepan and turn heat to high.

Cover and bring to boil. When steam starts to escape, turn heat to low.

Simmer covered for 10 minutes.

Turn heat off and leave to sit covered for another 10 minutes.

Remove lid and serve.

Risotto

Many believe that this dish takes great skill, but risotto is simple and forgiving. The quantity of broth required here is a little vague, as it will depend on how long it takes the rice to cook through, how much liquid evaporates, and, most importantly, how creamy or thick you like your risotto. I tend to heat about 5 cups of broth. When that runs out, I use boiled water from the kettle until I reach the consistency I like. You'll need:

>   2 tbsp olive oil
>   1 tbsp butter
>   1 medium sized onion, diced very small
>   1 cup arborio rice
>   1/2 cup white wine (optional)
>   5–6 cups of broth
>   1/2 tsp salt or to taste (depends on your broth)
>   1/2–1/4 cup grated fresh Parmesan cheese

Warm broth in separate pot on the stove, or boil kettle if using cubes.

Heat oil and butter in heavy saucepan on medium high heat. Sauté onion until clear.

Add dry rice and coat with oil. Allow to heat through without browning.

Pour in wine and stir, allowing alcohol to burn off and retain the wine flavor.

Ladle in broth and stir rice until almost all of the liquid is absorbed.

Stir and slowly add liquid with ladle as rice absorbs it. Sprinkle in salt.

Remove from heat when rice is soft to the bite, or *al dente* (about 20 to 30 minutes).

Toss in grated Parmesan cheese, stir, and serve.

Pass a bowl of Parmesan around the table to sprinkle on top.

There are many things that you can add to a risotto; you just have to know when to put them in. Hard vegetables should be put in at the beginning, or they'll be too crunchy. Good vegetables to add after the onions include carrots, butternut squash, pumpkin, asparagus, kale, spinach, fennel, and beets—basically, whatever appeals to your taste buds! Cut hard vegetables very small so that they cook through.

Good things to add near the end include grilled or smoked chicken, sausage, cooked seafood, and anything else you just want heated through and not overcooked. Choose your broth appropriately.

Tomato and Pesto Risotto

One more great idea, and my absolute favorite risotto recipe. There are some robust flavors in this one. Serve with an arugula or endive salad and a good bottle of wine when guests come over. You'll need:

2 tbsp olive oil
1 medium sized onion, diced very small
1 cup arborio rice
1/2 cup white wine
5–6 cups chicken or vegetable broth
1 can diced tomatoes and their juice (approximately 14 oz)
1/2 tsp salt or to taste (depending on broth)
6–8 chopped sun-dried tomatoes (packed in oil)
4 heaping tbsp pesto
1/4 cup grated fresh Parmesan cheese

Warm broth in a separate saucepan.

Heat oil in heavy saucepan on medium high heat. Sauté onion until clear.

Add dry rice and coat with oil, allowing to heat through without browning.

Pour in wine and stir, allowing alcohol to burn off and retain the wine flavor.

Ladle in broth and stir rice, allowing liquid to be absorbed.

Alternate diced tomatoes and their liquid with the addition of broth. Add salt.

Stir and add liquid as it absorbs. Add chopped sun-dried tomatoes.

Remove from heat when rice is soft to the bite, or *al dente*.

Mix in the pesto and grated Parmesan cheese. Serve with additional cheese at the table.

Brown Rice with Lentils

This recipe is inspired by many Middle Eastern dishes, but is made with brown rice for its health benefits. The nutty flavor of brown rice also works well with the lentils and nuts. If you prefer parsley to coriander, go ahead and substitute. Or, add 1 tsp of ground coriander. You'll need:

> 3/4 cup brown rice
>
> 1/2 cup green or blue lentils
>
> 2 tbsp vegetable or canola oil
>
> 3 green onions chopped, keeping green and white parts separate
>
> 1 medium-sized carrot diced tiny
>
> 1/3 cup chopped fresh walnuts
>
> 1 tsp ground cumin
>
> 1 tsp salt
>
> 1/4 tsp cayenne or to taste
>
> 1/3 cup raisins
>
> 1/4 cup fresh chopped coriander

Rinse rice and lentils together.

Boil in lots of hot water. The lentils should simmer for about 20 to 25 minutes

Test that they are cooked by tasting. (Overcooked lentils will turn to mush—they should be firm and the rice *al dente*.)

Heat oil in a large heavy bottom frying pan.

Sauté white parts of green onions and carrots for 5 minutes.
Add walnuts and spices and cook for a few more minutes until toasted, but not browned.
Remove from heat and add raisins.
Drain rice and lentils in a sieve. Rinse quickly without cooling too much.
Toss rice and lentil mixture in with items in the frying pan and mix gently but well.
Sprinkle with coriander and serve.

Rice Paper Spring Rolls

When choosing the appropriate size of rice paper disks to buy, consider how you plan to serve the rolls. For *hors d'oeuvres*, it makes sense to use the smaller disks, since when rolled up they're easier to handle politely and you only need to dip them once. Even better to cut them in half and expose the colorful filling. If you're making the rolls for lunches and are wrapping them in plastic, the large ones work just as well—like a closed up wrap sandwich. You'll need:

> 1 package rice paper disks
> fresh coriander
> butter or Boston lettuce
> green onions
> salted peanuts
> grated carrot
> matchstick-sized pieces of sweet red peppers
> matchstick-sized bits of any of the following:
>> grilled chicken
>> omelet-style egg
>> grilled tofu

Preparation is key. If you're organized before you start, you'll find them a breeze to assemble.

Prepare all of the ingredients you'll put into the rolls.
Fill bowl large enough to fit rice paper disks with very warm salty water.
Set up your assembly line as follows:
- package of disks
- large bowl with very hot salted water
- clean tea towel to lay disks on when soaked
- platter with all of the filling ingredients

102

- platter for the final product

Soak two or three disks at a time in hot water.

Remove carefully, without ripping delicate papers, and lay them flat on tea towel.

Place chosen ingredient in center of each circle.

Flip up bottom half of circle, then fold over sides into center and roll up.

Place on serving dish with the seam side down.

Serve with dipping sauce that follows.

Dipping Sauce for Spring Rolls

This is just one idea for dips that work with the spring rolls. You can make this sauce days in advance if you like. For an instant dip, or simply another option, buy "free" Chinese plum sauce at the supermarket and water it down. You'll need:

> 1/4 cup water
>
> 1/4 cup sugar
>
> 1/2 cup rice wine vinegar
>
> 1/4 tsp chili pepper flakes
>
> 2 tbsp chopped fresh coriander (optional)

Heat all ingredients (except coriander) in small saucepan on medium heat.

Stir until sugar has dissolved.

Cool and pour into one bowl or several small individual dipping bowls.

Potatoes

Potatoes originated in South America, where they were first cultivated by Inca tribes. They made the trip to Europe on Spanish trading ships, and soon became an important part of the European diet.

Hundreds of varieties exist in the world today. It's unlikely, however, that you'll be able to purchase potatoes that aren't grown regionally, so experiment with what's available to you. The starchy ones are good for baking or mashing. The waxy types are great for salads and recipes that call for grating or for cutting up for fries because they hold their shape well. When shopping, avoid soft, sprouting, green-skinned, or moldy potatoes. Store them in a dry, dark cupboard and avoid keeping them in plastic bags.

Roasted Potatoes

I learned to make roast potatoes with fennel seeds in Rome. The seeds add a very subtle, sweet licorice taste to the potatoes—but even friends who hate licorice love these. Rosemary can be used if you don't have the seeds. And the roasted garlic cloves are heavenly also. You'll need:

 6 fist-sized potatoes
 8 whole garlic cloves—peeled but not chopped
 1/4 cup olive oil
 1 tbsp fennel seeds or rosemary
 salt
 lots of fresh ground pepper

Preheat oven to 400°.

Chop potatoes into mouthful-size pieces, leaving skin on.

Toss in all other ingredients and coat potatoes.

Roast in oven, turning every 15 minutes for one hour or longer if you like them crispy.

Oven Fries with Skins

This is an easy and healthier way to enjoy French fries. I season these differently every time, depending on what I'm serving with them. The skins are good for you and leaving them on means less work! You'll need:

 4 fist-sized potatoes
 2 tbsp olive oil
 salt and pepper

optional (pick one):

 1/2 tsp paprika
 1/2 tsp curry powder
 1/2 tsp garlic powder
 1 tsp rosemary

Preheat oven to 425°.

Chop potatoes into very thin shoestring fries.

Toss in bowl with other ingredients to cover.

Spread on baking sheet and place in oven.

Turn fries after 15 minutes.

Bake another 15, or until desired texture and crispiness is reached.

Potato Latkes

These are a Jewish side dish made traditionally at Hannukah. For the crispiest latkes, you want the least liquid, the most starch and very, very hot oil to cook them in. If the oil is not hot enough, the potatoes soak up the oil, rather than being seared by it.

> 4 fist-sized potatoes, grated (skins are optional)
> 1 medium sized onion, grated
> 1 beaten egg
> 2 tbsp rice flour **or** 1 1/2 tbsp chickpea flour
> 1 1/2 tsp salt
> ground pepper
> 1/2 tsp baking powder
> vegetable oil for frying

Preheat oven to 350°. Prepare cookie sheet lined with paper towel.

Place grated potato in a piece of cheesecloth or a clean tea towel.

Scrunch cloth into a sack and squeeze excess liquid from potatoes into a large bowl.

Leave liquid to sit for 10 minutes. Pour off surface juice, reserving starch at bottom.

Mix the potatoes, which should be quite dry, back in with the starch.

Add onion, beaten egg, flour, and salt and pepper to potatoes and starch and mix well.

Heat oil in heavy frying pan.

Drop spoonfuls of the mixture about 3 inches apart when oil is very hot.

Flatten piles into little 2 1/2 inch cakes with the back of a fork or spatula.

Cook until crispy (about 4 minutes), then flip and cook other side.

Transfer latkes to oven to keep warm.

Serve with applesauce and/or sour cream.

Garden Latkes

Simply replace two of the potatoes with one carrot, one parsnip, and one small zucchini. Fresh dill also works well with this combination. Squeeze as much liquid out of the grated vegetables before mixing them with the potato and onion for a crispier result.

Upside-Down Potato Cake

A variation on a classic French dish, this potato side is lower in fat and cheese. This takes time to prepare (a good hour and 20 minutes in the oven), so save it for a weekend dinner or a leisurely weeknight.

> 4 fist-sized potatoes
> 2 tbsp olive oil
> 1 tsp Dijon mustard
> 3/4 tsp salt
> 1 tsp thyme
> fresh ground pepper
> 1/3 cup grated old cheddar or Gruyère cheese
> 1/4 cup broth (if not salty, add 1/4 tsp salt)
> butter

Preheat oven to 475°.

Slice potatoes into very thin rounds (leave skins on).

Toss in bowl with oil, mustard, salt, pepper, and thyme. Be sure to coat well.

Butter a 12" to 16" round casserole or quiche pan.

Lay half of the potatoes out in single layer overlapping.

Sprinkle cheese between layers and finish with layer of potatoes.

Pour broth over dish and dab with butter.

Cover with foil and bake for one hour. Remove foil and bake for another 20 minutes.

Remove from oven. Slide knife around edge to loosen.

Invert onto a platter and serve.

Corn

Corn is native to North and South America. It's just as popular today in many other parts of the world, where you might hear it referred to as maize.

When shopping for corn, look for cobs with dark kernels—the darker the corn, the more flavor it has. Corn on the cob tastes its best when it's barbecued with the husks still in place. Boiling makes the kernels absorb too much water and much of its flavor is lost to the water it's boiled in.

Cook loose corn kernels in as little water as possible and let them steam rather than boil.

Flours milled from corn come in all kinds of textures and are used all around the world in cooking as much as baking. Corn flours and meals keep best in airtight containers stored in a dry cupboard or the freezer.

Corn Pone

Corn pone was originally made by indigenous North Americans, who mixed ground dried corn with water and cooked it on rocks heated over coals. This version requires no rocks, but instead adds an egg, salt, and some herbs. These are great for breakfast or dinner. They can also be eaten hot or cold and pack well for lunches and picnics. You'll need:

>   1 cup cornmeal
>   1 beaten egg
>   2 tsp salt
>   1 cup water
>   butter
>   tarragon **or**
>   thyme **or**
>   chili powder

Combine cornmeal, salt, and beaten egg.
Add water and beat with fork until blended.
Melt butter in hot frying pan and drop batter by spoonful.
Shake pan to flatten out a bit.
Sprinkle herb or chili on the wet side of the pone—you can even vary them if you like!
Flip when browned and cook other side.
Serve with garnished side up on plates.

Polenta

Polenta hails from the north of Italy, but various forms of this basic dish can be found around the world. A shallow bowl of soft and buttery comfort is perfect on a blustery evening. Pass it around the table as a main course, ladling a simple tomato sauce or spicy lentils on top. You'll need:

>   8 cups clear water or broth
>   2 cups cornmeal
>   2 tsp salt

    6 tbsp butter
    1/2 cup freshly grated Parmesan cheese

Boil water in a deep, heavy-bottomed saucepan (polenta will bubble and spit).

Pour in cornmeal and salt in a slow and steady stream (a measuring cup with spout helps).

Stir constantly with a wooden spoon to avoid lumps.

Turn heat down to medium and keep stirring.

Push any lumps against the side of the pot with the spoon to break them up.

Continue stirring for about 20 minutes. Grains should dissolve and polenta will thicken.

Add the butter and cheese. Stir for another 2 to 3 minutes.

Pour into buttered casserole dish, or onto a wooden cutting board if cutting up.

Serve immediately with sauce, **or**

Allow to set on board, cut into squares or triangles, and grill or fry in hot pan with olive oil.

Polenta will keep for weeks if it's wrapped well and kept in the refrigerator.

Grilled Polenta

Polenta is extremely versatile. Simply slice up the "pasta" into squares or triangles (about 3/4 to 1 inch thick) and grill or fry in a pan with a little olive oil. Serve as a side.

You can also top with tomatoes, tomato sauce, pesto, sun-dried tomatoes, mozzarella, fresh Parmesan, goat cheese, fresh herbs, and olive oil. Use whatever you've got! Place squares on a cookie sheet and heat in the oven at 375° for about 5 to 10 minutes (watch them). Small garnished squares also make great appetizers for cocktail parties. Just add a stick!

Cheese and Onion Corn Bread

This hearty loaf is wonderful served fresh from the oven with chili or soup for dinner. Keep tightly wrapped and the leftovers will be great for lunches. You'll need:

    1 cup cornmeal
    1 cup corn flour

> 1/4 cup sugar
> 1 tbsp baking powder
> 3/4 tsp salt
> 1/4 cup soft butter
> 1 cup milk or milk substitute
> 2 beaten eggs
> 1/4 cup grated Parmesan cheese
> 4 chopped green onions
> 1 tsp chili powder

Preheat oven to 375°.

Combine all dry ingredients except cheese and chili powder.

Cream butter in mixing bowl and gradually mix in dry ingredients.

Pour in milk and add eggs. Beat with electric mixer until smooth.

Add cheese, onions, and chili powder.

Pour into buttered loaf pan.

Bake for 30 minutes.

Cool 10 minutes before removing from pan. Slice and serve.

Corn Tortillas

Tortillas can be purchased in any Latin American grocery store, but making your own is easy and rather satisfying. They're best when served warm and fresh. If they're not being enjoyed immediately, keep them covered and at room temperature. Tortillas can be eaten as bread alongside a meal or as wraps for sandwich fillings, or used as part of many Latin recipes. You'll need:

> 2 cups *masa harina* (fine ground white corn flour)
> 1 1/4 cups cold water
> 1/4 tsp salt

Mix water slowly into *masa* with a fork until it forms little clumps.

Knead dough on the counter sprinkled with *masa* for about 5 minutes until smooth.

Add a tiny bit of water if dough doesn't hold together well.

Divide into 12 balls rolling tightly in palms.

Flatten balls between waxed paper into 1/8-inch-thick disks. Trim with knife into circles.

Peel off of paper and transfer into dry heated skillet.
Cook on medium high until edges start to curl, then turn and heat other side.
Store under a damp towel in warmed casserole dish until ready to serve.

Buckwheat

Buckwheat, which is a grass, not a grain or wheat as the name implies, originated in Asia, and traveled to Russia during the Middle Ages where it became a dietary staple known as kasha.

Buckwheat can be bought natural or roasted. The roasted "grain" is soft brown in color and has a wonderful nutty flavor and aroma when cooked. When it hasn't been roasted, it can be lightly toasted in a dry skillet before cooking to enhance the flavor. Buckwheat is a very versatile food. Once the groats are cooked, they can be used for pilafs, stuffing, salads, or just steamed and enjoyed plain.

Any controversy regarding buckwheat has been due to concerns about cross contamination. Sometimes, buckwheat is milled in the same facility as wheat flour. If this worries you, find out more about where your buckwheat is coming from.

Steamed Buckwheat

I absolutely love the flavor and texture of steamed buckwheat as is. I'll even eat it at room temperature with no seasoning straight from the bowl as breakfast or lunch. Serve it hot with meat or fowl for dinner and add nuts, dried fruit, and soy or milk to the leftovers for breakfast the next morning. You'll need:

      1 cup toasted buckwheat
      2 cups water
      1/4 tsp salt
      1 tsp butter or oil

Boil water, salt, and butter.
Add buckwheat, cover, and reduce heat to medium, cooking for 10 minutes.
Remove from heat and leave covered for 5 more minutes.
Uncover, and fluff with fork.

Buckwheat Burgers

You don't need to be staying off the carnage to appreciate this nutty burger. Being very meat-like in texture, these burgers are a perfect way to make use of leftover buckwheat. Your family won't even recognize them as the grain they enjoyed the night before. Enjoy them in place of meat, or as a side with chicken and a salad. You'll need:

> 2 cups cooked cool buckwheat
> 1/2 cup well-chopped walnuts
> 2 tbsp sesame seeds
> 3 tbsp brown rice flour
> 2 chopped green onions
> 1 tsp thyme
> 1/8 tsp cayenne pepper
> 3 tbsp soy sauce
> 2 beaten eggs
> olive oil

Combine all ingredients in large bowl.
Heat olive oil in hot skillet.
Scoop mixture with a 1/3 cup measure and pack it in tightly.
Drop carefully into oil and gently flatten with spatula.
Flip when brown and cooked through, 3 to 4 minutes per side.
Serve as patties—or on a "free" bun.

Millet

Millet originates in northern China, and looks like a collection of little round yellow seeds. It's very high in nutrients, easy to digest (even for those with rice sensitivities), and very alkaline—which is good for those with acidic systems. This makes it a wonderful choice for people with digestive disorders.

Millet can have a pilaf, porridge, or polenta consistency, depending on the quantity of water you boil it in.

Steamed Millet

Millet is a little tricky to get just right if you want to use it for pilafs. The aim is to keep the grains separated and not too mushy. If it does overcook the first time, save it and reheat it as a breakfast cereal in the morning with raisins and walnuts or almonds. You can also use it for the millet croquet recipe that follows. You'll need:

> 1 cup raw millet
> 2 cups water
> pinch of salt

Wash grains under cold water in a sieve.
Boil water.
Add grain and salt.
Cover and reduce to simmer. Cook 10 to 15 minutes or until all water is absorbed.
Fluff with a fork.

Millet Croquets

I tend to eat steamed millet "as is" the first meal, but I always make enough to enjoy the following day for breakfast, and as croquets for lunch. I don't get bored because each dish is distinctly different. For these, you'll need:

> 2 cups cooked millet
> 2 beaten eggs
> 3 chopped green onions
> 1/4 cup fresh coriander (optional)
> 1/2 tsp salt
> 1/4–1/2 tsp chili powder
> olive oil

Break up any clumps in cold cooked millet.
Mix in all other ingredients except oil.
Heat fry pan with oil to high temperature.
Scoop mixture with 1/4 cup measuring cup and carefully drop into hot oil.
Flatten gently with back of spatula. When browned, flip and cook other side.

Quinoa

Quinoa dates back to the Incas of South America. Pronounced "keen-wah," this light textured grain swells into almost translucent little balls that appear to have tiny tails. It's very high in protein and easy to digest. Remember to wash quinoa well before cooking as it has a bitter coating that acts as a natural pesticide. Quinoa can be enjoyed as a pilaf, stuffing, breakfast cereal, or salad.

Steamed Quinoa

> 1 cup raw quinoa
> 2 cups water
> pinch of salt

Wash grains under cold water in a sieve.
Boil water.
Add grain and salt.
Cover and reduce to simmer. Cook 10 to 15 minutes or until all water is absorbed.
Fluff with a fork.

Quinoa Tabouli

Tabouli is traditionally a Middle Eastern dish made with bulgar, which is cracked wheat, or couscous, which is a form of wheat pasta. If you don't have quinoa around, you can also make this dish using leftover millet. Quinoa tabouli should be made a couple of hours before you're ready to serve it so that the flavors meld. It holds up well in the fridge overnight if you want to make extras for lunches, picnics, and potlucks. You'll need:

> 2 cups cooked quinoa
> 4 Roma tomatoes
> 1/2 cup cucumber
> 2 green onions and/or 1/4 cup red onion
> 1/4 cup parsley
> 5 fresh mint leaves or 1/2 tsp dried mint
> juice from 1/2 lemon or lime
> 4 tbsp olive oil
> 2 cloves crushed garlic
> salt and pepper to taste

Chop vegetables and herbs into very small pieces and toss in salad bowl.
Combine all ingredients when quinoa is cool.
Toss and leave to sit for a couple of hours before serving.

Amaranth

Amaranth dates back to the Mexican Aztecs. It's very high in protein, but the tiny little seeds have limited side dish potential because they produce a more porridge-like consistency when steamed or boiled. In my opinion, it's still a good option for breakfast. Cook it exactly as you would quinoa or millet. You can also pop it on the stove in a hot, dry pan in small quantities to produce a crunchy, nutty breakfast cereal served with milk or soy.

Amaranth is more popular in flour form, and is combined with other flours in baking for its flavor and nutritional value.

Legumes

Beans, lentils, and chickpeas fall into this category. Not only are they a great source of protein and fiber, but they're also rich in B vitamins, which are very important for those on a "free" diet. You can buy them dry, and soak and boil them for mere pennies a meal, but buying them ready-to-eat from a tin makes them a terrific convenience food.

Chickpea and lentil flours are widely used in Indian kitchens. Bette Hagman swears by bean flour in her newest books for baking bread. Bean flours are a great way to cut down on refined carbohydrates while increasing your fiber and protein intake. Once you try cooking and baking with bean flours, I'm sure you'll be hooked. A variety of bean flours are available in East Indian grocery stores and health food shops.

Chickpea Patties

These little patties are a variation on a West African dish. Not unlike the pakora, they can be deep-fried or pan-fried in very shallow oil. Chickpea patties are very easy to make and are high in protein, making them substantial enough to have as dinner with a salad. You'll need:

> 1 onion, finely chopped
> 1 19-oz can of chickpeas, drained and mashed
> 1/3 cup peanut butter (preferably natural)
> 3 tbsp corn flour
> 1 egg, beaten
> 1/4 tsp baking powder
> 1/2 tsp chili powder

1/2 tsp salt
oil for frying

Heat a little oil in skillet and fry onion until soft.
Mix soft onions in bowl with everything else.
Shape dough into 2-inch patties about 1/2 inch thick.
Fry in oil until brown and crispy (about 3 to 4 minutes), then flip
and cook other side.
Serve warm or cold.

Black Bean Cakes

This recipe is a cross between the chickpea patties and potato latkes.
They're fast and easy, so my guess is that you'll be making them a lot.
Don't be afraid to experiment with other seasonings. Because they're
excellent reheated in a dry pan, you can double up the batches and have
them later in the week, too! You'll need:

1 grated fist-sized potato (leave the skin on)
1 cup drained and rinsed black beans (turtle beans)
2 tsp cornstarch
3 chopped green onions
1/4 cup fresh whole cilantro leaves
1 clove garlic, minced
1 tsp chili powder
1 tsp cumin
1 tsp salt
fresh ground pepper
1 egg beaten
olive oil for frying

Mix all ingredients in a bowl.
Heat olive oil in hot skillet.
Drop batter into very hot oil, making flat 3-inch rounds.
Flip when underside is golden (about 4 minutes).
Keep warm in oven on paper towel-lined baking sheet.

Vegetable Pakora

Pakora are usually found as appetizers on Indian restaurant menus. Deep-
frying will result in fritters. Frying them in just a little oil will make little
pancakes, which are not as traditional, but still make a tasty side dish. I

115

doubt you'll have leftovers, but if you do, reheat them in a dry frying pan on medium high and they'll be just as yummy—if not better! You'll need:

1 cup chickpea flour
1 tsp salt
1/2 tsp baking powder
1 tsp ground cumin
1 tsp ground coriander
1/2 tsp tumeric
1 tsp garam masala
1/4 cayene pepper
3/4 cups water
1/2 tsp mustard seeds
1 medium onion, sliced into thin rings
1 fist-sized potato with skin on, sliced very thinly (approx 1/16" rounds)
2 cups chopped fresh spinach
canola or vegetable oil for frying

Mix first 8 dry ingredients together in a bowl and add water to form batter. Let sit.

Heat 1 tbsp oil in non-stick fry pan (with lid) on medium high.

Sauté onion and mustard seeds. Add potatoes when onion is clear. Sauté for 5 minutes.

Add 1/4 cup of water. Stir and cover to steam-cook potatoes.

Turn down heat. Stir occasionally until potatoes are soft but hold together well.

Remove from heat and let cool down a bit.

Mix into batter and stir in spinach, coating all ingredients.

Wipe out pan, return to heat and pour in more oil.

Spoon mixture into approximately 3-inch rounds when oil is very hot.

Lift around sides as they start to firm up. Flip when underside is golden brown.

Fry other side until batter is cooked through.

Remove and drain on absorbent paper. Keep in warm oven until ready to serve.

Pakora can be made with other kinds of vegetables or even just onions alone. Experiment with what you have in the house.

Cassava/Tapioca

Cassava, which is native to tropical countries, has a brown outer skin and is white inside. Sometimes the very center is a little stringy or woody; otherwise it's similar to a very starchy potato. In North America, the food is most commonly known for its role in tapioca pudding. This particular pudding is made from tapioca flour, which comes from the cassava root. The flour is often used as a thickener, and can also be mixed with other flours in baking to add more spring to the food. Look for very firm cassava in large grocery stores or in ethnic shops of tropical origin.

Boiled Cassava Root

A very simple food. Try it with a light fish dish for a change from potatoes.

Peel and then cut the root lengthwise into quarters or sixths.
Boil in plenty of salted water.
Remove any stringy bits that run down the middle of the vegetable.
Serve with butter and salt, or mash as you would potatoes.

Plantain

Plantain is most popular in the warm climates where it grows. The plantain is similar to a banana, but it contains considerably less sugar than our dessert variety and is used more like a starchy vegetable than a fruit. Plantain can be prepared when it's ripe or unripe. Unripe plantain has firm flesh and green skin, whereas the ripe fruit is yellow with black streaks, and is a little sweeter. It can be boiled in the skin, mashed, baked, or fried.

Golden Plantain

This is very fast, easy, and sure to become a family favorite. Plantain cooked this way goes great with fish, rice, and beans, or even eggs for breakfast. It's also good as a snack, and can be eaten cold. In the Dominican they like to deep-fry it, but I find that it comes out just as nicely when it's fried in less oil. Don't be too skimpy though, or the plantain will be dry. You'll need:

unripe plantain (green or yellow—but without black streaks)
canola oil for frying
salt

Peel plantain and slice it on the diagonal into 1-inch-thick chunks.

Fry in hot oil, cooking both sides until golden.

Remove from oil and flatten pieces on a board using the bottom of a glass.

Return to oil and fry for a couple more minutes.

Sprinkle with salt and serve.

Baked Plantain

Plantain is a fairly dry vegetable, so you'll need to add a little fat during the cooking process. This very simple recipe is sweet and aromatic. Plantain is a very filling food, so I usually base quantities on half a plantain for each person if it's accompanying substantial portions of anything else. You can remove the plantain from its skin before you serve it, or let the diners eat it out of the skin on their plates. You'll need:

ripe plantain (yellow with black streaks and no green)
1 tbsp butter per plantain
1 tsp sugar per plantain
cinnamon for sprinkling

Preheat oven to 350°.

Cut ends off plantain and slice down the middle to form boats.

Place in an oven-proof baking dish and add thin slices of butter alongside the openings.

Sprinkle with sugar and cinnamon.

Bake for 30 minutes.

Serve in skins, or remove skins before transferring to plates.

More Vegetables as Carbohydrates

What better way to get your family to eat more vegetables than serving them as you would a starch? Try these ideas instead of potatoes or pasta.

Caribbean Baked Sweet Potatoes

What makes these sweet potatoes so special is the texture of the coconut. These are a hit with kids and could almost be served as dessert! Sometimes I cook more sweet potatoes than I need. I serve simple ones *au naturel* the first night, and then scoop out and stuff the leftover ones later in the week. You'll need:

> sweet potatoes
> 1 tsp butter per potato
> 1 tbsp flaked or shredded unsweetened coconut per potato
> 1/2 tsp cinnamon per potato (substitute 1/4 tsp ginger and 1/4 tsp nutmeg)

Preheat oven to 350°.

Wash sweet potatoes and place in oven-proof dish.

Bake for 30 to 40 minutes (until soft). Remove from oven and let cool a bit before handling.

Cut potatoes in half lengthwise. Scoop centers into a bowl (keeping skins intact).

Mash centers with cinnamon and coconut and return to potato skins. Dot with butter.

Return to oven and warm through for 10 minutes, or reheat if using cold potatoes.

Spaghetti Squash as "Noodles"

Spaghetti squash are yellow or tan colored and oblong in shape. When cooked, the inside can be scraped out with a fork to form slightly crunchy spaghetti-like strands. Look for larger ones for the best flavor and the biggest strands. These instructions are for the oven, but you can also cook them in the microwave (cut in half, cover with plastic wrap, and cook for approximately 15 to 20 minutes on high). You'll need:

> 1 spaghetti squash
> 1 tbsp butter
> 1 tsp salt

Preheat oven to 400°.

Cut squash in half lengthwise.

Dot with butter and sprinkle with salt.

Place in baking dish with foil on top.

Bake for 30 to 45 minutes (depending on size). They should be soft when tested with a fork.

Remove and scoop out strands lengthwise with a fork.

Serve under stir-fried vegetables or sprinkled with salt, pepper, and Parmesan cheese!

Pasta

While I have tried to avoid including recipes that come from the world of gluten, I must admit that my move back to Italy means that on occasion, one must partake in a plate of pasta. The following are two classic, simple sauces to enjoy with good-quality gluten-free pasta. (See below for suggested brands.)

For best results, cook pasta in lots of boiling water with a good dose of salt. Read the cooking instructions on the package. Just before the suggested time is up, test to ensure it's not *cotta* (overcooked). This is especially important with the gluten-free variety. It should have some bite, or be *al dente*. Finally, never rinse pasta—the sauce won't stick. Make the sauce in a large skillet and mix in the drained pasta before serving.

Pasta Arrabbiata

Arrabbiata translates to "angry"—referring to the "heat" or spiciness of the sauce. You can control this with the quantity of crushed chili flakes that you use. This recipe is really easy, has very few ingredients, and serves 4. You'll need:

> 3 tbsp good-quality extra virgin olive oil
> large clove of garlic
> 1/4 tsp to 1 tsp crushed dried chilli pepper flakes
> large can peeled or crushed tomatoes and their liquid
> dash of salt
> 1/4 cup chopped fresh parsley
> gluten-free pasta of your choice

Heat olive oil in large non-stick skillet.

Smash garlic with back of knife.

Place garlic open side down in oil along with crushed chili flakes.

Remove garlic when golden (not burnt).

Add can of tomatoes and their liquid.

Cover and leave to cook on medium high.

Stir occasionally.

Add a little water if tomatoes start to stick.

Cook until tomatoes are completely broken down (about 20 minutes).

Remove sauce from heat and cook pasta in lots of boiling water.

Return sauce to heat when pasta is ready.

Add a dash of salt to taste and fresh parsley.

Drain cooked pasta and stir into sauce.

Pasta Carbonara

Normally, Italians eat a plate of pasta and then they eat dinner. Seriously.

When offering only pasta, we opt for something a little heavier and complete. This is my favourite pasta dish, but it's not for calorie counters. Serves 4. You'll need:

> 3 tbsp good quality extra virgin olive oil
> 1 large finely diced onion
> fresh ground pepper
> 12 slices chopped raw bacon or 3 pork sausages broken up into little pieces
> one glass dry white wine
> 2 medium eggs
> 1/2 cup roughly grated fresh Parmesan cheese
> gluten-free pasta of your choice
> salt to taste

Heat olive oil.

Cook onion until clear with a good dose of black pepper.

Toss in bacon or sausage pieces and stir until cooked through.

Sip and then pour wine into skillet.

Stir until wine has burned off.

Remove skillet from heat.

Whisk eggs in bowl and set aside until pasta has cooked.

Drain pasta and toss into skillet.

Return to high heat for 2 minutes.

Stir in egg and quickly toss around pasta (to avoid scrambled eggs!).

Sprinkle with grated cheese, stir again, and serve immediately.

These days, the variety of pasta available worldwide is incredible, and the quality is so good. I have yet to dine with a Roman who hasn't been surprised by the authenticity of the following recommended brands available in North America. (Check out the websites to learn more about distributors in your area.)

Dr. Shär (Italy)
Large variety of pasta, each made with a different combination of gluten-free ingredients including corn, rice, and soy.
www.shaer.com

Molino di Ferro (Italy)
Corn pasta and organic corn pasta
www.molinodiferro.com

Tinkyáda (Canada, made with American rice)
White and brown organic rice pasta
www.tinkyada.com

Nutricia Glutafin (Spain)
Combination of corn, rice, potato, and soya
www.glutafin.co.uk
search: distributors

Pastariso, Rice Innovations (Canada)
Organic rice pasta
www.riceinnovations.com

A Sample Gluten-Free Menu

The seven-day menu below illustrates what an ideal, healthy, gluten-free diet looks like in real life. There are lots of gluten-free bread, pasta, cookie, and muffin options for those days when you simply must eat on the run. This plan is based on natural, healthy foods, rather than the processed, pre-packaged foods available on the market. No matter what's available in your neck of the woods, you are not completely dependent on gluten-free suppliers. Lunches are organized with eating away from home in mind.

Recipes follow this sample menu plan. An asterisk indicates an opportunity to cook once and use the grain or dish in a variety of ways (as leftovers or as part of other recipes) within the week. (An asterisk placed before food means make extra for a later meal. An asterisk placed after food means this is a leftover from a previous meal.)

Day 1

BREAKFAST

3/4 cup low-fat plain yogurt with half a sliced banana and 1/8 cup fresh walnut pieces

MID-MORNING SNACK

Pear or other half of banana from breakfast

LUNCH

White Bean, Tuna, and Tomato Salad with rice crackers
4 Peanut Butter Cookies

MID-AFTERNOON SNACK

1/4 cup raw or roasted unsalted almonds

DINNER

*Roman Stuffed Tomatoes
Baked White Fish
Lemon Spinach

Day 2

BREAKFAST

2 slices gluten-free toast with almond butter
Hot soy milk with cinnamon

MID-MORNING SNACK

Applesauce or fruit cup (in juice rather than syrup)

LUNCH

Roman Stuffed Tomatoes (can be reheated or eaten cold)*
Chickpea Salad

MID-AFTERNOON SNACK

1/4 cup trail mix

DINNER

*Lemon Roast Chicken with Potatoes
Steamed broccoli

Day 3

BREAKFAST

Scrambled or soft boiled egg with gluten-free toast or
reheated leftover potatoes*
Sliced tomato

MID-MORNING SNACK

Individual fruit yogurt

LUNCH

Piece of roast chicken (can be reheated or eaten cold)*
Hummus with slices of red pepper, cucumber, and carrot
sticks

MID-AFTERNOON SNACK

Half an avocado with salt and pepper on rice cakes

DINNER

Grilled Salmon
*Brown rice
Steamed green beans with butter, salt, and toasted
sesame seeds

Day 4

BREAKFAST

Bowl of *buckwheat, brown rice*, millet, or quinoa (serve cold or warmed with raisins, walnuts, or sliced almonds, sprinkle with cinnamon, and pour gluten-free soy milk on top)

MID-MORNING SNACK

Applesauce

LUNCH

Salad: bed of Boston lettuce with small can of tuna in olive oil, half an avocado, sliced tomatoes
Hard boiled egg dressed with olive oil and/or lemon, salt, and pepper

MID-AFTERNOON SNACK

4 Peanut Butter Cookies

DINNER

Buckwheat Burgers with Oven Fries

Day 5

BREAKFAST

Cheese and/or tomato omelet with slice of rice toast

MID-MORNING SNACK

Banana

LUNCH

Buckwheat Burgers (can be reheated or eaten cold)
Tomato and Cucumber Salad with Feta Cheese

MID-AFTERNOON SNACK

1/2 cup toasted almonds or cashews

DINNER

> *Homemade Chili* with soft corn tortillas or nacho chips

Day 6

BREAKFAST

> "Poached" Pears with Ginger or Cinnamon with plain low-fat yogurt

MID-MORNING SNACK

> 1/4 cup roasted sunflower seeds

LUNCH

> Homemade Chili with nachos*

MID-AFTERNOON SNACK

> Piece of fruit

DINNER

> *Zucchini Soup*
> Grilled cheese sandwich

Day 7

BREAKFAST

> Low-fat cottage cheese with sliced fresh or canned peaches (in juice)

MID-MORNING SNACK

> 6 dried apricots and 1/4 cup raw or toasted almonds

LUNCH

> Zucchini Soup*
> Rice crackers or cakes with your favourite cheese

MID-AFTERNOON SNACK

Air-popped popcorn

DINNER

*Tomato and Pesto Risotto with salad on side

Recipes

Lemon Spinach

1 bunch fresh spinach
2 tbsp olive oil
juice from 1/2 lemon
salt

Wash spinach and chop into pieces.
Heat oil in large skillet.
Toss in spinach.
Stir until wilted.
Squeeze in fresh lemon juice.
Sprinkle with salt and serve.

White Bean, Tuna, and Tomato Salad

1/2 can white kidney or cannellini beans (drained and rinsed)
1 individual serving can of tuna in olive oil (or half a regular size can)
1 tomato chopped into small chunks
salt and pepper

Combine all ingredients in a bowl. If there is insufficient oil with the tuna, add some good-quality olive oil.

Peanut Butter Cookies

1 cup peanut butter
1 cup sugar
1 egg

Combine sugar and egg.

Mix in peanut butter.

Form into small balls approximately 1 inch in diameter.

Place balls on an ungreased cookie sheet, flatten with fork.

Bake for 10 minutes at 325°—be careful not to over bake.

Cookies taste better on the second day.

Roman Stuffed Tomatoes

> large round tomatoes
> 2 tbsp Italian style or Arborio rice per tomato
> 4 large oblong potatoes, peeled
> fresh basil or oregano
> 1 tsp olive oil per tomato
> salt and pepper

Carefully slice the tops off of the tomatoes and put aside for later.

Scoop out the insides of tomatoes along with their liquid, and place in bowl.

Break tomato insides into small pieces and add salt, pepper, basil, or oregano.

Add rice and olive oil.

Put mixture back into tomatoes and replace tops.

Cut each potato into 6 lengthwise wedges and mix in bowl with oil, salt, and pepper.

Place tomatoes in casserole dish that holds them snugly.

Replace tomato tops on tomatoes

Stand potatoes on end and wedge between tomatoes. This keeps tomatoes from breaking apart, and potatoes take flavour from tomatoes.

Bake in preheated oven at 350° for 1 hour.

Simple Baked White Fish

> 1 3-lb whole fish for 4 people or a few smaller fish for individual servings (try porgy, red snapper, gilthead—or ask at your local market for the best fish available in your area)

olive oil
garlic
dried rosemary
salt and pepper

Clean fish.

Cut open lengthwise, keeping fish intact.

Gently rub chopped garlic, salt, pepper, and rosemary inside.

Make aluminum packets for each fish. (Fold the foil over the fish and crimp the ends.)

Place on oven rack (seam sides up) and bake for approximately 45 to 60 minutes (depending on size and thickness of fish) at 350°. Smaller individually wrapped fish will cook in about 30 minutes.

Test with fork. Fish should flake easily when fully cooked.

Chickpea Salad

1 can chickpeas (drained and rinsed)
2 carrots diced very fine
1/2 red pepper diced very fine
1 green onion chopped very fine
1 tsp chili powder
juice from 1/2 lemon
3 tbsp olive oil
salt and pepper

Combine all ingredients in bowl. Allow to sit for 2 hours for best flavour. Makes enough for 2 to 3 side servings.

Lemon Roast Chicken with Potatoes

1 whole chicken
10 small new potatoes
1 lemon
rosemary
olive oil
1/2 cup white wine
salt and pepper

Clean chicken, rub inside and out with salt, pepper, and rosemary.
Squeeze 1/2 lemon inside chicken.
Place in baking or roasting dish.
Cut potatoes in half (leave skins on).
Place potatoes around chicken, round sides down (so they don't stick to pan).
Sprinkle with salt, pepper, and rosemary.
Drizzle 1/4 cup olive oil over potatoes and chicken, pour 1/2 cup white wine over chicken.
Place in oven preheated to 375° for 1 hour to 1 1/2 hours (depending on size of chicken).
Baste every 15 minutes with baster or spoon using juices that escape from bird.
Add water in small doses if pan appears dry to avoid a burnt or dry chicken.
Turn potatoes halfway through.
Squirt other half of fresh lemon over chicken and potatoes before serving.
Makes enough for 3 or 4 servings, plus a lunch for next day.

Hummus

> 1 can chickpeas (drained and rinsed)
> 1/4 cup tahini (sesame paste)
> 1/2 lemon
> 3 cloves garlic
> 3 tbsp water
> 1/4 cup olive oil
> salt and pepper

Combine all ingredients in a food processor.
Mix until paste is very smooth.
Serve. Keeps when well-covered in the refrigerator.

Grilled Salmon

> salmon fillets
> juice of 1/2 lemon
> olive oil
> salt and pepper

Place fillets in glass baking dish, skin side down.
Add salt, pepper, lemon, and olive oil.
Place on rack under broiler and watch carefully.
Cook 4 to 6 minutes and turn, cook other side 4 to 6 minutes.
Test with fork. Fish should flake easily when fully cooked.

*Buckwheat Burgers

See page 111.

Oven Fries with Skins

See page 104.

Tomato and Cucumber Salad with Feta Cheese

2 to 4 tomatoes, depending on size (hothouse, Roma, or whatever is freshest or in season)
1/2 seedless English cucumber
1/4 cup crumbled feta cheese
1 tsp dried oregano
1 tbsp olive oil
salt and pepper to taste

Combine all ingredients. Makes enough for one lunch serving.

Chili

1 large diced onion
1 tbsp olive oil
1 lb lean ground beef
1 large diced red pepper
1 can rinsed black (turtle) beans
1 can rinsed red kidney beans
1 large can peeled tomatoes and juice
1 1/2 tbsp chili powder (or to your taste)
1 1/2 tsp salt
optional hot chili flakes for additional spiciness

Heat olive oil in large, heavy saucepan.
Sauté onions until clear and add red pepper.
Add ground beef and cook until browned.
Add chili powder, beans, and tomatoes.
Stir and cover.
Cook on medium high heat.
Stir occasionally. Let simmer for 1 1/2 hours.
Freezes well for future meals and lunches.

"Poached" Pears with Ginger or Cinnamon

> 2–3 ripe pears
> ground ginger or cinnamon
> 3 tbsp water

Peel pears and slice into thin wedges.
Arrange in single layer in skillet.
Add water.
Cover with lid.
Place on medium heat to steam.
Remove from heat when cooked through, sprinkle with ginger or cinnamon.
Cover another 2 minutes and serve with yogurt.

Zucchini Soup

> 1 medium onion, diced
> 1 tbsp olive oil
> 4 large zucchini, sliced thinly
> 1 medium potato, peeled and diced
> 2 tsp dried thyme
> 1 vegetable or chicken bouillon cube
> boiling water as needed
> 2 bay leaves
> 1/4 cup chopped fresh parsley
> salt and pepper

Heat olive oil in medium large saucepan.
Sauté onion until clear, but not brown.
Add zucchini, stirring until half cooked.

Add thyme and potatoes.

Stir and drop in bouillon cube; add boiling water until ingredients are just covered.

Add bay leaves.

Bring to a boil and then let simmer 45 minutes.

Remove bay leaves and add fresh parsley, salt, and pepper to taste.

Allow to cool and place in blender (or use hand blender in pot), blend until smooth.

Reheat and serve.

Tomato and Pesto Risotto

See page 100.

These recipes should help to keep things new and exciting for quite some time. Of course, no matter how adept you are in the kitchen, there are times when playing "chef" or "dishwasher" isn't so appealing. Restaurants can seem a bit daunting at first, but a read through chapter 9 will soon have you ordering someone else to cook the dinner!

9

THE RESTAURANT

Table Manners

Dissecting Your Food

There are almost 1,800 restaurants listed in my local Yellow Pages directory. Yes, I counted. I have probably only ever eaten in 25 of them. I really ought to get out more.

If a restaurant is new to me, the first thing I do before stepping foot inside is look for a menu posted outside. If there isn't one, I ask the *maître d'* to show me a copy before I'm seated. While contemplating the prices, I look for the kinds of foods that I know can be rustled up gluten-free. If they only serve pizza and pasta, I look for another place to dine.

I took such steps one evening at an Italian restaurant that was new to me. I perused the menu posted in the vestibule with a friend and shook my head. Moments later, the owner called after us down the street to ask why we had left. When I explained why I couldn't eat anything but a salad on his menu, he offered to make me any pasta dish they served—with rice noodles. This man did not need my business; the restaurant was packed. As a matter of fact, my friend and I had to wait 20 minutes at the bar for a table, but I didn't mind one bit. Any restaurant that's ready to accommodate *and* chase me down the street has my business.

There are times when a meeting place is prearranged by friends or business associates. If you have a chance, call the establishment ahead of time to find out what kinds of foods they serve. Explain your situation and ask them what they would suggest within these parameters. (Keep reading this chapter for suggestions about what to ask for over the phone.) These steps can save you from having to make a big production at the dinner table. I would also suggest that you make this call during non-peak hours so that you can get the full attention of a staff member.

Once you're seated comfortably in the restaurant and you have established what is safe for you, you'll be faced with the breadbasket. Inevitably, the server will place it directly in front of you, especially if you're painfully hungry. The irony is that this will happen when the restaurant is very busy and trying to buy your patience. Accept that the bread will be fresh-baked, warm, and aromatic. This is the way of the world. Hand it over to your dining companions—who will feel guilty for their genetic abilities—and order yourself a drink. Let's take a look at the appetizers, shall we?

Starters

Generally, the simpler the food, the less you have to dissect. Salad is safe, without croutons. As for dressing, higher-end restaurants will usually make their own. You can ask that they use their dressing if the chef is confident that it's "free." If not, opt for olive oil and balsamic vinegar or a wedge of lemon.

Soup will require a few more questions on your part. Is it a cream soup? Is it thickened with flour? Is there any pasta or barley in it? Does the chef use a homemade broth or a bouillon? Ask every time, as the head chef might do it one way and the sous chef another. Conversely, you might want to consider whether any bowl of soup is worth so much investigation.

Appetizers require that you beware of breaded things. Calamari can be grilled with lemon and oil, but it can also be battered and deep-fried. Spring rolls can be made with cold rice paper or deep-fried flour wraps. If anything isn't clear on the menu, ask. Even if it seems clear, *ask*. (Looks like the server is going to earn his or her tip tonight.)

Mains

The entrée can be a little trickier as you're often dealing with more than one food group on a plate. Here, you'll need to learn to read carefully, and get over any inclination to be timid, since you'll definitely be asking more questions. First, look to see if something is stuffed, coated, or floating in sauce. If, for example, the chicken is stuffed with goat's cheese and spinach, chances are good that it's *prestuffed*—meaning that if breadcrumbs are part of the equation, you can't have the chef omit them. And even if the fish or chicken says pan-fried with a lemon butter sauce, don't assume that this means *just* lemon and butter. The fish could have been dredged in flour before going into the pan, meaning that particular sauce is fairly open to interpretation. Find out how something is made. If you're skeptical of the staff's comprehension of your concerns, ask that your entrée be broiled, baked, or grilled with herbs or fresh ground spices.

And if the entrée you want comes with pasta, look further down the menu to see what the other mains are served with. If, for example, the sirloin comes with a baked potato or the salmon comes with rice, it should be no big deal to substitute one of these sides for whatever is supposed to accompany your entrée of choice. This really isn't a lot to ask. Do make it known that you have a food intolerance and not a fussy disposition. Ask the server to write on his or her order to the kitchen: NO FLOUR or NO GLUTEN: SERIOUS ALLERGY or CELIAC DISEASE. You can also carry a card in your wallet and ask that the server show it to the kitchen staff who will be preparing your meal. The server is sure to be more understanding if he or she knows about the seriousness of your condition. You're relying on him or her to relay your requirements to the kitchen staff. If you don't trust that the server is capable or caring enough, strut back to the kitchen. Even threatening to do so might help paint a clearer picture. Respect yourself. If an establishment thinks you're too painful to cater to, don't bother with it. Your patronage will be appreciated elsewhere.

I should also point out that if you order something and it arrives appearing suspicious, don't be afraid to go back to the kitchen to clarify what they've put on your plate. If the message didn't get through to the kitchen, and you didn't get what you asked for, give it back. You have every right. There's a place in my neighborhood that will serve up a gluten-free pizza. Every single time I order it, I very clearly tell the server that I want the gluten-free version, and every time it arrives at my table, I'm suspicious because *it looks so good*. Friends have become used to my ritual walk to the back of the restaurant to check up on the server by asking the person who made my pizza directly if it was, in fact, gluten-free. It's all in how you handle it—and I'll get into more detail later.

Your Celiac Association chapter may have spent time educating restaurant owners in your area. Find out if they've compiled a list of restaurants that have been familiarized with gluten intolerance. If your

Association has not tackled this, you might suggest that members share their experiences in the chapter newsletter. You could start by sending in your own report on where you've been and how you've been treated. Your Association should be able to provide you with restaurant information cards to keep in your wallet; if not, copy the one that follows.

Desserts

You're stuffed, you can't eat another bite—unless, of course, it's dessert. As I'm sure you've already discovered, this section of the menu is often pretty barren for us. I love ice cream, and don't mind popping lactose pills so that I can enjoy it. Look for homemade gelato, tartufo, sundaes, fruit cups, and sorbets. Sometimes you can find crème brûlé, custards, and rice pudding. You can always ask the kitchen to put some of the caramel sauce intended for the apple crumble on your chocolate gelato. While you're at it, why not just ask if they can whip you up a little something special in their kitchen? Sometimes, I get the best dessert at the table. Otherwise, opt for a fancy coffee and virtuously watch your friends' waistlines expand.

Put It in Writing

The following card is for passing to the kitchen when ordering food at a restaurant. You might want to keep an extra supply of these in the glove compartment of your car. Shrinking and laminating this wouldn't be a bad idea either, as trips to the kitchen can be messy.

I have Celiac Disease and MUST NOT eat any foods containing GLUTEN.

Gluten is found in wheat, rye, triticale, barley, oats, and malt. Even the smallest amount can make me very ill.

Please avoid serving me anything:

- Coated, dredged, breaded, or containing flour or breadcrumbs
- Made with bouillon cubes, or processed soup or gravy bases
- Processed in any form, as these foods may contain gluten (e.g., soy sauce, miso, salad dressings, and seasoning mixes)

Contamination can also occur on a grill, pot, or with utensils.

Please do not place my food in a fryer used to cook battered foods.

Your attention and assistance in providing me with a safe meal is greatly appreciated.

Traveling Around the Block

How much ethnic diversity you have to choose from will naturally depend on your neighborhood. If you want more variety on a menu, frequent restaurants that feature cuisine from cultures where the staples are rice, corn, or potatoes rather than wheat.

As usual, you'll be asking a lot of questions. This time, however, you may find yourself asking them of people to whom English is not a mother tongue. Gluten is not even a word that many *English*-speaking people are clear on. I would suggest that you copy the restaurant card provided and tuck it in your pocket before you go just in case. It's also worth repeating the value of making a phone call during non-peak hours before you venture out, if this is your first visit. Make the first reservation for a quieter night of the week, so that there will be staff around who can afford to take time and chit chat about the menu with you.

Ethnic restaurants typically offer lots of "free" options, so have a look at the following.

Thai Restaurants

The first Thai dish I ever tried was Pad Thai, which is made of thick rice noodles and bean sprouts with shrimp, chicken, egg, and tofu in a sweet and spicy tamarind sauce with crunchy sprouts and peanuts sprinkled on top. Yummy.

The next discovery was the cold rice paper spring rolls filled with vegetables, coriander, and rice noodles. The rolls are safe—just find out what the restaurant provides for dipping. If you're wary of ordering off of the menu the first time for fear of ingredients used in the sauces, ask for a double order of these rolls and you'll be more than satisfied.

Although a couple of the noodle dishes are wheat, most Thai dishes are rice- or rice-noodle-based. Thai food is fiery, sweet, citrus, and salty. Fresh coriander is used extensively, as are chilies, ginger, lemongrass, and fish sauce. So you see, most Thai dishes are quite complicated, mixing many ingredients to achieve the magical effect. Though most also use simple, unadulterated natural ingredients, do verify that any flavorings are free of fermented sauces that use wheat. Fear not. There should be more options than there will be opportunities to try all of the dishes that are available to you!

Indian Restaurants

Indian restaurants use chickpea and lentil flour in many of their dishes. Look for papadum, which are flat, cracker-like breads, or pakora, which are vegetable fritters made of chickpea flour. In restaurants that serve South Indian cuisine, you'll find baji, which are very similar to pakora. Vada, another deep fried snack, are often "free"—but only if they're made from ground split peas. (Do verify what else is being fried in the oil tonight.) Dosas are huge savory pancakes made of lentil and rice flour, and are folded over a mixture of curried potatoes. And we're still just on the appetizer list.

For entrées, pick from the endless mélange of chickpea stews, curries, dhal, lots of spicy vegetable dishes, and the best basmati rice pilafs. Forget about the breads and the vegetable cutlets, as they're made with wheat flour. Indian restaurants also use yogurt in some dishes for its cooling properties. If you can tolerate lactose, order a lassi, which is a yogurt drink that will help to cool your palette. I'll risk redundancy by telling you once again to ask the server to clarify that everything you order is safe for you. I'm confident, however, that you'll be giddy with the variety you can safely choose from. See what they have to offer in the way of dessert, as many are made with milk, sugar, and chickpea flour. If I were you, I'd find out about the desserts before ordering your meal, as you may want to leave some room!

Japanese Restaurants

Sushi restaurants are not just for those brave enough to ingest raw fish. On my first visit, I didn't eat any raw fish at all. They serve great sticky rice and California rolls—which are made of rice mixed with bits of vegetables rolled in a seaweed wrapper, called nori. But beware of the soy sauce and tamari, which are used extensively. However, the wasabi, which is a green mustard made from horseradish, may feel like it's burning holes in your nostrils, but it won't hurt your villi.

The more elaborate Japanese restaurants serve up a variety of fresh vegetables and meats on a grill right before your eyes (what better way to know what you're getting?). These are worth a phone call ahead of time, since you can ask them to prepare your food without wheat-thickened soy, tamari, or teriyaki sauce, or see if they would mind using your wheat-free stuff from home.

As for noodle dishes, be sure that yours are made with rice flour. Both udon noodles and soba noodles are made with wheat. Soba noodles are sometimes referred to as buckwheat noodles—don't be fooled.

Both saki (rice wine), and the plum wine served in Japanese restaurants are gluten-free. Just make sure you ask that soy question before *you* get sauced.

Chinese Restaurants

The Chinese buffet may look like a smorgasbord of gluten-free opportunities; sadly, however, this just isn't the case. What looks like rice and vegetables is undoubtedly smothered in soy sauce, and the soy sauce in most of these establishments is made with wheat flour. If it's not called soy, it's called tamari or teriyaki—which for your purposes just means more potential wheat. Before you start piling up your plate, find out more. And if you're highly sensitive, watch those buffets where serving spoons are being used to serve gluten-laden dishes. You might want to pass on the specially priced all-you-can-eat buffet and opt for a safe dish from the kitchen, where the staff has been made aware of what to keep off your plate. You may end up with less to choose from, but the pay-off is worth it. If they're open to using your soy sauce from home in their kitchen, hand it over! If not, you can bring some with you to add at the table. It's your good fortune that the paper is the best part of those cookies they serve at the end. You can save your villi—and your dental work—by leaving the tasteless shards on the tablecloth.

Latin Restaurants

Mexican cuisine is often based solely upon corn and rice dishes, making it another very celiac-friendly option.

Tortillas are flat breads that can be made either with corn or wheat, and are a staple in many dishes. Whenever you order a dish that reads tortilla, ask what that tortilla is made of. You can also ask if the kitchen would be willing to substitute the corn tortillas for wheat ones in a particular dish. If this is not an option, ask the server to clarify which items on the menu are made with corn tortillas. Always *clarify* that they are wheat-free, and also ask about any sauces, chilies, etc., that may possibly contain flour as a thickener.

The Spanish are famous for their paella, which is a rice dish made with chicken and shellfish, and flavored with saffron and other spices. Spanish and Cuban restaurants often feature a tapas menu, providing a great opportunity to dabble in all kinds of "free" dishes, which are sized like appetizers. Check out the selection of fresh seafood dishes—some are served with cassava or yuca, which is a boiled tuber vegetable similar to a baked potato, but with a unique texture and woody flavor. Also look for sweet baked plantain or crispy fried plantain. And after you've asked all the pertinent questions about your food, hand over your car keys and order a jug of sangria.

Italian Restaurants

Italian restaurants should not be written off. The pasta and pizza joints should be avoided unless, of course, you're not averse to bringing your own bag of pasta or a pizza crust for them to top. Keep in mind that you'll need to request that they use fresh boiling water, clean baking trays, etc. (there's a lot of flour floating around in a pizzeria!).

Full menu restaurants offer some decent options: antipasto plates, grilled calamari, salads, or clear, homemade soups without noodles. Also look for risotto or polenta in the pasta section of the menu. Risotto will usually have Parmesan cheese in it, and will sometimes be made with cream as well, but *neither* is necessary for a good risotto. This is a dish that's never made in advance, so ask that the chef make you a lactose-free version if you can't tolerate milk products. My time in Italy taught me that you need be clear that they are not using boiled water from the pasta pot to make the risotto. Many meat dishes look pretty safe, but this doesn't mean that you shouldn't ask the server for details. Italian recipes are often chock-full of bread crumbs, and you'd be surprised at how many times I've asked if something has flour in it and have been told *no*. When I then asked about breadcrumbs, I was told *yes*. And where do breadcrumbs come from?

As for dessert, you're only in luck if you can stomach milk. Ask about zabaglione, gelato, tartufo, or budino di riso. If you can't do the milk and can't go without something sweet after dinner, be a traditionalist. In an Italian home, fruit is always offered at the end of a meal. You just never know what they've got in the kitchen!

Greek Restaurants

When I emailed the Austrian Celiac Association for suggestions about good places to eat in Austria, the woman who responded directed me to a Greek restaurant.

Tell the server to keep in mind what you can't eat, then order a variety of dips and watch him or her carry over a platter of hummus, babaghanouj, tzatziki, tapanade…the options are endless. If you ask nicely, they'll even bring you a plate of healthy cucumber slices instead of the pita bread that is normally served alongside these dips. If this is lunch, you might even want to stop there.

Another great starter is dolmates, which are grape leaves wrapped around ground lamb and rice. If you're looking for calamari, make sure you get the grilled and not the battered and fried version. Consider the calories you've just saved yourself while you squirt your dining partner with fresh lemon.

How inviting it is to see almost every entrée arrive at the table with a side of both rice *and* roast potatoes! In this Mediterranean land, your best bet is to order the simplest of foods. Grilled meats like souvlaki with the aforementioned heap of carbohydrates and salad are usually wise choices, and there is almost always a good selection of grilled fish to choose from. Some of the more complicated dishes like moussaka are made with béchamel sauce, and are therefore not a very good idea. Don't get so wrapped up in flirting with those Mediterranean servers that you forget to ask the appropriate questions!

There are, of course, as many different types of cuisine as there are cultures in the world. Within the cultures I've covered, there are infinite versions of the dishes mentioned, since the families that run the bistros that serve them hail from different regions that incorporate unique twists into each recipe. Work on your conversational skills and find out more about what culinary pleasures *your* neighborhood has to offer!

Being High Maintenance

I can't count how many times I've repeated the mantra "Ask Questions." Now, I'm going to suggest that you ask people for help, rather than telling them what to do. Asking someone to help you makes them feel valued. No one bends over backwards for someone they don't want as a return customer, and a little charm and a polite demeanor can sometimes get you the best service in the dining room.

If the restaurant is extremely busy and the person waiting on you looks particularly busy, you might want to approach your requirements a little differently. This probably isn't the best time to ask what the server recommends off of the menu, or the best time to send him or her back to the kitchen three times with questions. Make yourself easy to take care of.

144

Use your best judgment as to what looks safe. When you order, simply ask the server to let the kitchen know that you can't eat gluten in any form. Ask the server to write this on the actual order, and hand him or her an information card if you have one. I would also suggest that you give the server another choice from the menu in case the first can't be prepared without gluten. If the chef has a question or concern, the server can come back and see you.

If I have made a special request on a very busy night, I also try to be more patient. I would rather that the cooks pay attention to what goes on my plate during a lull on the line. (Ideally, you have called the restaurant to let the staff know of your needs at reservation time. This isn't a guarantee, but it does give the chef some time to think about you before you get there.)

And don't forget the power you wield with a tip. We forget that a tip is a way of saying you appreciate the good service. The kitchen staff don't get the same kind of reward, so if it's an open kitchen I'll make a point of saying thank you for a lovely meal. Otherwise I'll ask the server to pass on my compliments. Finally, remember that it's called the *hospitality* industry for a reason, and a restaurant is only as good as its reputation. With so many restaurants for us to choose from, celiac patrons need only dine with the best.

Drive Right on Thru

Now if only we could say the same for take-out food. One of the doctrines of the last century has been that faster is better. This has done nothing for our diets but provide a lot of boring food to a lot of sluggish people. For those of us who aren't genetically predisposed to digesting meals composed of cardboard and grease, the take-out phenomenon will provide one of the biggest challenges of all.

I lived on a diet of French fries for years. Thick, thin, extra crispy, with or without skins...until they came up with those coated/seasoned things, I really thought I had the fast food dilemma beat. But hey, what do teenagers know? Grease is the word. In a fish and chip shop, for example, the fries are cooked in the same oil as the battered fish. Many fast food places make onion rings in the fryer, and McDonald's uses theirs to fry pies. The only truly safe fries are made from nothing but potatoes and fried only with fellow spuds (the irony being that those greasy French fry trucks may be your healthiest option).

When you absolutely must drive-thru, pray that they have a take-out salad or a baked potato. And do your homework. You might be willing to eat the hamburger patty (sans bun) if you know that the chain doesn't put fillers in the meat *and* if it never comes in contact with a bun.

Don't put your health in the hands of a high school kid who isn't likely to grasp the gravity of your situation. In an emergency, try the Asian food court establishments when you're in the mall. To ensure that what you're getting is safe, ask for the plain rice rather than the fried rice. If they don't have it out, surely they have some in the back. Chances are, the vegetables are cooked with the same gluten; if so, see if they have anything steamed (or raw) in the back that has yet to be doused. Like I said— emergency measure.

Fast Food Take-Out Options

- French fries if they're not coated and the oil isn't contaminated
- Salad box with side of packaged dressing that you can verify is safe
- Baked potato with butter (not "topping") and chives, salt, and pepper
- Chinese food (the food part—hold the gluten-laden soy sauce)
- Barbecued chicken (as long as it's basted in sauce that's "free")
- Corn tacos without any processed cheese sauces
- Grilled chicken sandwich—hold the bun
- Hamburger patties that are made without fillers

Your local Celiac Association chapter will likely have a list of what each major chain offers in the way of gluten-free foods. This information alone is worth the annual membership fee!

Less Mainstream Take-Out Food Options

Travel beyond the Golden Arches. You'll find many options in the health food store take-away counter. (It's refreshing to pick up food from a place that can actually tell you what's in the food!) Also, get to know the independent places that offer take-out in your area, and look for take-away options like:

- Sushi and California rolls with wasabi mustard
- Cabbage rolls in spicy tomato sauce
- Souvlaki skewers
- Curries
- Roasted potatoes and roasted vegetables
- Green salads

- Rice salad and potato salad
- Bean, lentil, and chickpea salads

When faced with one of those sandwich bars that only serves salad as an option, try asking that they combine the sandwich filling offerings with the salad for a more substantial meal. For example:

- Grilled chicken breast on a bed of salad
- Tuna salad or egg salad on a bed of greens
- Chopped sliced meats like pastrami, chicken, or turkey (if they can confirm that they're gluten-free)
- Chopped slices of mozzarella or swiss cheese

Get to know where you can find these options to alleviate panic when hunger sets in. Try your best not to leave home empty handed if you know you're going to be trapped in a mall or know you won't have time to scout out food. We call fast food "junk" food for a reason. Most of what you can't eat is very bad for everyone's health. At least you'll eat a lot less of it!

Now that we've got you eating outside of the house, you must be ready to interact with the gluten-eating populace. Look to chapter 10 for tips on graciously getting your gluten-free needs met in a variety of social scenarios.

10

THE SOCIAL SCENE
Life Skills

In the middle of difficulty lies opportunity.

—*Albert Einstein*

A Piece of Cake

The birthday party is the social scene of the prepubescent set. The appropriate gift as seen on TV must be offered up, the birthday boy or girl must be ungrateful and unwilling to share, and bad behavior all around is fueled by the intake of too many refined sugars administered by the party coordinators.

These events just may be the training ground for future ravers and substance abusers. As a parent, it's your responsibility to ensure that your child is appropriately socialized and can function within these battlefields. Despite the handicap of being unable to participate in the hot dogs and birthday cake, you must arm your child to the best of your ability, without being too conspicuous.

All joking aside, it can be traumatic for a child to feel left out or different in a way that makes him or her unable to participate. It is, of course, necessary that your child fully understand the gravity of the situation—all the while knowing that you understand how she feels. It's really a balancing act between paying full attention to your child's needs and making everything appear to be as normal as possible.

My mom was pretty good at handling birthday parties. I ate hot dogs, too. Mine arrived with a toothpick in them so that the host would know which ones were "free." I also had my own bun. (Not so inconspicuous—you should have seen rice bread in the '70s.) I doubt this happened every time, but I do remember her supplying a meringue shell to be filled with ice cream and strawberries in lieu of the cake, making the other partygoers a little envious of *me* for a change.

There was usually a discreet conversation between my mother and the host before the festivities to cover all of the bases. When time permitted, my mother would provide a safe treat for me to bring and share with the others. If this sounds like a good idea to you, you might want to consider keeping some cupcakes or treats stashed away in the freezer to alleviate last minute panic.

Some suggest that you ask the parent hosting the party if you can supply the birthday cake, allowing your child to participate as well. I'm a little wary of this, however, as it can lead to confusion with a small child. It also means that you end up making a cake every time, which is not always possible—or okay with the other parents. Because these occasions will arise, you'll have to explain to your child each time whether or not he can eat the cake, and this can be confusing. I believe that it's better to keep the rules simple. Your child will appreciate a special cake on his birthday all the more.

If you're a grown up, I don't think I need to go over any strategies for coping with birthday cake withdrawal. Stop pouting and go pour yourself a nice glass of wine—it's a much better use of the calories anyway!

The Beer and Pizza Party

Pizza is my enemy. It keeps turning up whenever I'm with a group and the closest means of being fed is via the telephone. I might sound a little melodramatic here, but I've found myself feeling close to tears when a pizza is being ordered, especially when I'm hungry. Yet ordering the pizza is truly a tribal ritual. There's the organizing of the toppings, collecting of the money, timing of the delivery...democracy in action. It's one of the only times I feel quiet and insignificant amongst the group. Actually, more accurately, I feel invisible and kind of pathetic. My true self feels like screaming and throwing a tantrum. *How can these people be so insensitive?*

I used to be a real martyr. I used to act like it was okay to order it and gorge in front of me while I sipped on a soda, secretly feeling miserable.

Despite my attempts to act like it was no big deal, my secret usually oozed out of me in the form of resentment or sulky behavior. I became a child. But I don't want sympathy. I also don't want to feel guilty for depriving the "normal" people from their natural ability to eat the freakin' pizza. I want empathy. I want them to see right through the tough facade and order chicken instead.

Sometimes, for reasons beyond explanation (even to you), you find yourself wanting to attend parties that you *know* will revolve around pizza and beer. Should your masochistic side win, you can prepare for the challenge.

Bring a tray of something you can eat—like a veggie platter with hummos, or nachos and salsa. This way everyone is eating some of what you're eating, making you feel less singled-out by what's on your plate. In my opinion, anyone who invites you to this kind of soirée should know enough to consider doing this for you anyway. Don't take any chances. There's no such thing as too much food when we're talking about *your* options.

You may even want to bring your own pizza, and put it in the oven when you get there. If the host is actually making the pizza, just let him or her know in advance that you'd like to bring your own crust to be topped. (Check your health food store's freezer for a shell you can pick up on the way to the party.) Should you opt for loading it up when you arrive, be sure to verify that the ingredients made available are "free." For example, pepperoni and pre-grated cheese are common hideouts for gluten.

As for the beer, drink wine. Show those barbarians that you've got some class. Every Italian knows that you drink wine with pizza!

The Watering Hole

Unless you want to stick to wine, you need to learn a bit more about alcohol before you step up to the bar. I've always felt a little intimidated in drinking establishments. It's not just the pick-up scene that mortifies me, but all of those bottles behind the bar void of ingredient listings on their labels. And really, why are we expected to know what gin is, while all of the secrets of cornflakes are revealed right on the box? Isn't it incredible to think that with all of the concern over the safe use of alcohol, most people can't even tell you what's in a bottle of gin? My concern took me to meet with the manager of Quality Control for the Liquor Control Board of Ontario.

In Canada, there are very strict regulations and standards for alcohol products brought into the country. There is a list of guidelines for labeling; though ironically, manufacturers don't need to put the ingredients on that label. I'm told this is because of the nature of how alcohol is made. One year the distillery may use corn because it's cheaper that season than wheat. And a winery may change the combination of things they put in the wine based on the grape crops in any given season. I'm told that it's a very expensive undertaking to track the exact ingredients and their quantities on every label. Imagine if the makers of cornflakes were given the same leeway?

Alcohol consumption raises issues that cause a lot of grief for people with grain intolerance, since associations and medical practitioners around the world have different opinions about what's safe and what isn't. I spent the first 30 years of my life believing I should avoid anything that's been distilled from grains. Now, I've learned about research that proves these forms of alcohol are safe. Unfortunately, I've already been conditioned, and it's difficult to wrap my head around swallowing something I once thought was the equivalent of rat poison. You may want to do some research of your own.

There are two different processes for making alcohol: fermentation and distillation. Very simply put, fermentation is the addition of yeast to a sugar (like grapes). Yeast acts on the sugar, creating carbon dioxide and alcohol. Beer and wine are both made this way.

Distillation begins with the addition of an enzyme to starch, which creates sugar. Yeast is then added, and the result is fermented alcohol. The liquid containing this alcohol is then heated. The alcohol, which contains very small molecules, evaporates faster than the other liquid in the vat. The actual grains used to make this product are protein molecules too large to evaporate with the alcohol. So the grain remains in the "mash" or mush left in the bottom of the vat. The result is pure alcohol with none of the characteristics of the product from which it originated. To this end, a distiller of vodka can use corn one year and wheat the next and the product will not change. Gin is also made in this manner, but what makes it different from vodka is an infusion of herbs and flavorings.

The reason it's important to note the difference between these two processes is because in fermentation, the ingredients all go into the bottle. In distillation, only the vapors from the ingredients are returned to liquid form, and thus go into the bottle. These molecules are not carrying any of the grains used to make the by-product. It's been suggested that the quantity of gluten left after the distillation process is so minute that you would have to drink an entire barrel of whiskey to experience any side effects. However, in that case, I don't suspect you'd notice a reaction to the grain.

Because I grew up believing that it wasn't safe for me to drink alcohol made from grains, I only drank grape-based alcoholic beverages. I recently learned that these very beverages I'd been consuming for years are in fact fortified with neutral spirits (grain alcohol). But I'm still here, and my latest biopsy indicates no damage.

I do respect that you may be skeptical, so here's a guide to where alcohol comes from so that you can decide for yourself what you're comfortable with.

Made from fermented grapes:
- Wine (red, white, and rose, ice wine, dessert wine)
- Brandy
- Cognac (French)
- Grappa (Italian)
- Tsipouro (Greek)
- Port

Made from fermented apples:
- Calvados

Made from fermented plums:
- Japanese plum wine

Made from fermented grapes, but may be fortified with distilled neutral spirits:
- Cinzano
- Campari
- Dubonnet
- Vermouth (martini)
- Port

Made from fermented rice:

- Japanese saki

Beer is definitely out. No point breaking this to you gently: there are no substitutes made gluten-free; if you're at a pub, order a cider instead. Cider is fermented like beer, but made with apples.

Alcohol distilled from neutral spirits:

These are usually corn, wheat, or a combination of both. They are used because they are inexpensive. Barley, rice, or potatoes may also be used.

- Vodka
- Gin
- Rye
- Whisky

Alcohol distilled from products other than grains:

- Rum is distilled from sugar.
- Vodka *can* be distilled from potatoes, and will be labeled as such if it is.
- Tequila is distilled from a cactus called blue agave; however, only 51 percent of its contents need to be distilled from this to qualify the product as tequila. The other 49 percent is usually grain alcohol (neutral spirits).

Things get a little trickier with liqueurs. It's safe to say that most are made with neutral spirits (grain) as their alcohol base. A few products on the market, like Grand Marnier, Godet, and Poirot are made with cognac. The bigger problem, however, lies in the *other* ingredients in the bottle. Distillers of alcohol are not currently required to list the ingredients used to make the product on the label. If you have a favorite and would like confirmation that it's "free," I suggest you contact the distributor for more information.

One very positive thing I did learn is that the Canadian government is starting to look seriously at the plight of allergy sufferers. People with life-threatening allergies are leading the crusade, and this is going to help everyone. Soon food and alcohol products sold in Canada will be following codes for clearer labeling of high risk allergens such as nuts, milk, eggs, seafood, soy, wheat, and sulfites. In Canada, alcohol is filtered through Liquor Control Boards. For more information on specific alcoholic products, or to get the names and phone numbers of their distributors, call your provincial liquor control authority.

In America, contact the Bureau of Alcohol, Tobacco and Firearms (ATF). The ATF is a federal bureau in Washington, DC. One of its many functions is the definition and regulation of alcoholic beverages. They can be accessed via their website, at *www.atf.treas.gov.* (Be prepared to wait for an answer to your questions in writing.)

Your newfound confidence and wealth of knowledge might just lead to some very interesting conversations with attractive strangers.

Kiss—But Don't Tell

Your first date with a potential partner can be very indicative of the relationship's chances for survival. Inevitably, it will be suggested that you go out for dinner, followed by some discussion as to where you'd like to go. Now, there are two ways you can handle this. One way would be to clear your throat and go into the whole "schpiel" about how you're ridden with disease, and how it's not contagious, and hello? Are you still there? The other way would be to suggest a couple of restaurants that you've established as hassle-free. No need to divulge your reasons for choosing a place.

First dates are full of first impressions, and there's absolutely no reason to paint a "limited" picture. You're not holding out on any information that should make a difference. Show your date how adventurous you are (you are, aren't you?) and suggest that you go to some out-of-the-way East Indian place you know. See how this could work in your favor? If your date finds this tedious, you'll save yourself a lot of time.

I'm not saying that your needs should be given the slip, I'm saying that a high maintenance first impression is not necessary to ensure that the date will be able to work with your lifestyle. I once dated a guy who called the restaurant he wanted to take me to for our six-month anniversary so he could check out the menu. He actually talked to the chef to be clear on what was gluten-free, freeing me, I might add, of the rigmarole that eating in a new place usually brings. It was probably my most romantic celiac moment (can't you just hear the violins?). Keepers figure it out in good time.

Don't turn what should be romantic into a "celiac moment." Why make a big a deal about what you don't eat when there's no need to "go all the way" on the first date? Your "strange" diet can only add to your mystique. You know how to take care of yourself, and I'm sure that there are more interesting things you can share about yourself than the state of your small intestines. Save that fascinating conversation for date number three.

155

I Do and I Don't

I figure that eventually one of those dates is going to lead to a wedding. But chances are (unless you're Liz Taylor) you'll be the guest at more of these events than you will the host, so we'll start there.

Any time we're confronted with a pre-set menu, panic sets in. The standard party hall menu usually consists of rubber chicken in some congealing, beige sauce, side pasta, and wilted salad. (Admittedly, I'm cruel—but often it really is just a small step up from hospital food.) And even if it is a posh affair, a limited menu is just that. Realizing that brides-to-be already have their heads full of other important affairs—like cummerbunds and taffeta gowns—there are some things you can do to take care of yourself on "the big day."

In all honesty, I used to just eat something before I went. If it was going to be a long day, I'd shove something in my purse and scarf it down in private. You can always use this plan while in training mode, but I find that it only contributes to that left-out feeling. And the bathroom is really no place for dinner, especially when you're all dressed up.

A few years ago I was a guest at my friend Valerie's wedding. We hardly ever saw each other any more, and I hadn't reminded her about my diet. When my plate arrived I couldn't believe that she had made the effort to ensure it was served up "free." When she came over to make sure that all was in order, I was overwhelmed with gratitude. It's a small thing, but her empathy allowed me to avoid a drawn-out conversation with my dinner companions about why I was only eating the carrots on my plate.

When you're ready to take matters into your own hands, you can always slip a note in with those silly little reply envelopes where you divulge whether you're showing up alone or have scored a date. If you're buddies with the lucky aisle-walker, you could just call her to ask what's being dished up. This is also a great time to ask that you get seated with the fun people and not her great aunts. And if you really don't want to be a "pain," you can call the hall to find out what's being served. If it's not an up-charge to substitute, why not take care of matters yourself? A word of warning, however: it might be a good idea to let the bride know, or check with her first. Brides are highly sensitive to others meddling in their plans even when we have the best intentions.

In Sickness or in Health...

Finally, if you should decide to put on a big spread at your wedding, you can decide exactly what goes on the table. On your day, you can make it a "free" for all. Use this opportunity to set an example. Perhaps you can put a note in those reply envelopes asking if there are any dietary concerns that you can pass on to the caterers? No doubt you empathize with the angst some of your guests may feel about their food intolerance. My friend Leela had a lot of different dietary restrictions on her guest list, and decided on a buffet that addressed everyone's needs. There was even some rice bread. How about that?

And anyway, there are many caterers "catering" to those with dietary restrictions these days. It's become a big part of the market. We need to start fueling the trends that will eventually make life a lot easier for all of us.

The Dinner Ring

One Saturday afternoon, I was invited at the last minute as a date to a dinner party that same evening. I knew the host of the sit-down supper, but only as an acquaintance. This woman did not know enough about me to know that I was intolerant of gluten. Hours before the event I was overcome with panic. *What if the dinner was lasagna?*

I faced a dilemma. I could call her up and tell her about my diet, or I could just leave it alone and hope for the best. I felt guilty about being difficult. I felt afraid that she would resent being inconvenienced. I reminded myself that she hadn't *actually* invited me. Would I embarrass my date? If I didn't address the issue, and she served something that I couldn't eat, everyone at the table would be uncomfortable. I couldn't win. I was a wreck—the evening hadn't even begun and my stress levels were through the roof.

I tortured myself for a while before I decided what to do. If I hadn't known the host at all, I would have asked my dinner date to make the call. Seeing as I knew her enough to look her up in the book, I took the plunge myself. With a deep breath, I picked up the phone.

Dinner was to be some kind of chicken dish. So far, so good. I pushed the envelope a little further and asked how it was being prepared. The sauce was being thickened, but she said that she could substitute cornstarch if that was all right with me. Whew—close call (literally). Most importantly, she told me that she was relieved that I had checked in with her. She assured me that there was no need to be embarrassed, and she

157

thanked me for saving her from the discomfort that may have ensued had I not rung her up.

The moral of the story is that you're doing yourself—and the host—a disservice by not addressing your needs in advance. If you know what's being served, you can always make things simple by offering to help. If pasta is the plan, why not just bring a bag of your own. Boiling another pot of water is all they have to do for you to partake. If a side dish is decidedly going to be impossible for you, perhaps the host can throw a baked potato in the oven. If the fish is battered, ask that they fry yours up first *au naturel*. These are not big impositions.

Throwing your own dinner party is all about your mindset. Your biggest problem here might be worrying that you're denying your guests. Depending on my mood, I may put out bread with dinner, but in all honesty, that usually has more to do with the fear that I won't provide enough food than fear that my guests will miss their precious bread.

You might feel that your meal is so obviously missing gluten—probably because *you* are so conscious of it. But guess what? Gluten-tolerants don't eat wheat every night! And this is also a great opportunity to show off your culinary expertise! Why not delight your guests with one of the new exotic foods from chapter 7?

Finally, try to remember that while you're obsessing over all the details of what's offered up on the plate, most people are really only interested in having you at the table because they enjoy your company. So, sit back and relax!

The Unsuspecting Houseguest

I had a friend from Italy stay with me for five weeks one summer. For the first time in my life, I found myself loading Wonderbread into my buggy at my local grocery, because for Alessandra, this symbolized America. Yet in the five weeks that she stayed with me, those white enriched tissues were one of the only deviations that girl had from my everyday diet.

Alessandra had experienced nothing more ethnic than Chinese take-out food before her arrival. (The Chinese food place she frequented in Rome also served pizza—for the less daring Italian palettes.) During her stay in Toronto, we ate Indian, Thai, Mexican, Greek, Middle Eastern, and of course her favorite—junk food, which no one does better than North Americans. I don't eat hot dogs—which I couldn't rob her of—but she agreed to limit her hankerings for the tubes to the vendors of street meat when she was out roaming the city without me.

Alessandra was a tourist—admittedly easier to cope with than the likes of a local who expects to find certain "necessities" in the cupboard. The local I'm referring to here has been "the boyfriend." If food is the way to your man's heart, you *might* want to keep a couple of bagels in the freezer but, on the other hand, maybe his last girlfriend *only* offered bagels.

I don't bother keeping gluten-containing foods in my house, with the exception of a bag of toxic cookies. When guests drop by, I can put out a few cookies rather than really feed them. I'm incapable of keeping "free" cookies in my home for more than six hours, which means that there would never be any cookies left to share with the beloved guests. A bag of wheat-laden chocolate chip cookies, on the other hand, can rot in my cupboard for months without me even considering a nibble. Willpower? I doubt it. I just don't see those cookies as an option. It would be like snacking on a box of paperclips.

If you're concerned that it'll cause you angst, I strongly suggest you avoid having dangerous food around. When others enter your home, you shouldn't feel like you're depriving them of anything. And once you introduce them to the "free" world, there's a good chance that more interesting options will show up for you when you visit *their* homes.

Better Living

There's no need to suffer in silence. We *can* improve the quality of our social experiences if we start speaking up for ourselves in social situations. When the attitudes of those in our "inner circle" start to change, we feel more comfortable about advocating change outside of our comfort zone. So why not set an example? Take into account the fact that someone else within any given group may also have some food concerns. When suggesting a place to eat or food for a meeting at work, make sure that the food is tolerable to all concerned. If you want your needs considered, you need to do the same. This kind of behavior will soon become second nature to the people in your life. And the habit of asking questions *can* make life easier for a lot of people. It may be the stone thrown in the pond—the one with a ripple effect that benefits everybody.

And show your gratitude. When others go out of their way to take care of you— by, say, baking a special "free" cake, or buying rice crackers instead of wheat ones for the picnic, or ordering a special lunch in for the department meeting—say *thank-you*. You may also want to send a card to a friend or a memo to a coworker who considered your needs. Showing appreciation will inspire others to continuously perform good deeds.

159

The quality of our lives is really up to us—not our celiac disease. Using the disease as an excuse to live anything less than a full and fulfilling life is sad. Why not make it just another opportunity to care for and respect one another?

Finally, life is back to normal. As time passes, all the details that once seemed tedious will become second nature, and we'll end up looking after ourselves just fine. That said, it's time for the home stretch—or perhaps the away-from-home stretch as we travel to chapter 11.

11

THE EXCURSION

Getting Away with It

Life shrinks or expands in proportion to one's courage.

—*Anais Nin*

Sleeping Around

Be it a five-star hotel, a two-man tent, or your best friend's new abode in the next state, at *some* point you're bound to find yourself waking up to a new day somewhere else. Over the course of this next chapter, we're going to slowly extend your umbilical cord to reach new places, and learn how to deal with the specific challenges they may bring.

When you're planning to spend time at someone else's home, you can make yourself welcome beyond the "three day rule" by taking care of yourself. Bring a loaf of your own bread and perhaps some crackers or pasta. If I haven't had time to get organized, I'll ask the host where the local health food store is and pick up my sundries on the first day of my arrival. If I'm staying in a new city, I actually try to get into the health food stores anyway so that I can scope out offerings from the bakers in the area.

To help alleviate your host's anxiety about the food supply, let him or her know that you'll help out with meal preparation. This way he or she can learn a bit more about your requirements, and you'll know exactly what you're eating.

If it's not you, but Junior, who's off for a sleepover or a weekend at your in-laws, send along simple instructions. Remember that your level of outward anxiety can make things scary and uncomfortable for everyone. Clearly explain the diet to the host and leave him or her with a list of foods to avoid, or copy the card provided in chapter 9. Your child has to learn to survive amongst others without your supervision.

On the one hand, *we* need to make sure we don't eat anything that's going to make us sick. On the other hand, if we arm someone with the right information, eventually we'll be able to enjoy the luxury of having someone else take care of the cooking.

On the Road Again

Sitting strapped into a vehicle for long periods of time is more than many of us can endure. Eventually we all need to get out and stretch our legs, so when that sign symbolizing gas, food, and a place to pee appears, we often can't control the urge to pull over. Roadside diners usually provide eggs and home fries, omelets, burgers, and fries. My attitude is: when in Rome.... Basically, don't bother with healthy food in a greasy place. Look around—will a place that's comfortable serving coffee in stained mugs (complete with lipstick imprints) really bother to wash the lettuce for your salad? My second road trip motto is: Whatever doesn't kill me makes me stronger. An order of nachos covers all the food groups, right? (Hope I packed my vitamins.)

I like to travel, but I'm usually on a pretty tight budget when I do so. This isn't the best combination when you're trying to make healthy choices. Better restaurants with fresh ingredients usually offer more selection for those who don't want to fill up strictly on grease and carbohydrates. Better restaurants, unfortunately, cost more money. So you have to plan ahead. I'm a squirrel when traveling. I have bags of nuts, cookies, or crackers with me at all times. You might even want to consider a bake-off before the trip to provide yourself with individually wrapped muffins or banana bread.

And if you're not into carting food around, take some advice from the Boy Scouts, and be prepared. Packing the right tools can really make finding sustenance easier. These little things will easily fit into the side pocket of a daypack:

- Wet Naps
- Spoon and fork
- Can opener

- Paring knife or pocket knife. (A great way to carry a paring knife in your bag without getting hurt or cutting through the bag itself is to carry it in a plastic toothbrush travel case. You might want to pack a corkscrew too.)
- Small Tupperware containers. (Buy the ones that fit inside one another. Leave with them filled, and use them as dishes when buying food on the go.)

I'd suggest you try to budget for at least one nice and nutritious meal a day when you're on the road. You can help your pocketbook by picking up food at the local market or grocery store, and eating it on the go or in a park. Keeping a set of utensils and a paring knife wrapped up along with some wet naps in your bag lets you enjoy yogurt and applesauce or cut cheese and apples. And a can opener makes a tin of tuna as convenient as a slice of pizza! You'll eat better than if you hit a fast food operation two or three times a day—you'll also have more cash to offset the cost of a higher-end restaurant for dinner.

People with food intolerance can never really throw caution to the wind, and they tend to forget what it means to relax when it comes to their food. Don't be hard on yourself if every meal that you eat isn't a nutritious one. Most people are actually more laid back about their diet when they're away from home. If you eat like a teenager for a few days every now and again, it won't kill you. Just make sure you're a teenager with some celiac street sense.

Preparing for Take Off

What they serve on an airplane may look like hospital food, but for what it costs, it would be nice to be able to eat it.

Almost every airline has a special menu for diabetics, vegetarians, and those who require kosher meals; many also offer a gluten-free alternative. Usually, you have to call at least 48 hours in advance (which might explain why the food tastes so bad by the time it gets to you on the plane). But if you forget to call, or if it's a very short "snack" flight, make buddies on the plane and trade. You'd be amazed how many cheese slices and fruit cups you can get in exchange for one of those nasty little sandwiches. And if you're shy, simply ask the steward for extra peanuts. Sadly, many airlines have switched to pretzels or peanuts that have been adulterated in such a way that they're no longer an option. You may want to bring up the peanut issue when you're booking your special meal. Any chance they have gluten-free cookies?

Another crisis-management maneuver is to wait until all of the meals are served and then ask if they'll provide you with the surplus "free" goodies from the extra trays. A little politeness can take you a long way. And hey—I'm often told I got the better meal deal. But I can afford to be cocky about the food tray challenge, because I never leave for the airport without a bag of crackers, almonds, or cookies. I always travel with emergency rations. I just like to see what I can get on the plane. It's kind of a game for me—one I make sure I never *really* depend on.

Anyone taking a trip has to make arrangements before leaving. You simply have to add a few requests to the places that you book in order to fully enjoy the pleasures of travel. The more we get out there and make these requests, the easier it will be for all of us. We need to support the companies that are willing to support us. If a "service" company won't take care of our needs, we need to let them know that we won't be booking tickets for our family of six (go ahead, embellish) and why. Speak up, and create demand. I envision a time when the airline asks whether I have any dietary concerns, and when "free" focaccia and biscuits arrive on my airplane food tray.

Adventures in Eating

A foreign country is no place to get sick. Who wants to be stuck in a hotel all day while friends gallivant, only to sit up in pajamas listening to tales of their excursions when they return? People with serious food intolerance avoid travel outside of the safety zone that they've created for many reasons. We fear that we won't be able to find safe food, or the bathroom. Or we worry others won't understand our needs, or we'll have to cart around too much food—which, we then fear, will spoil. Doesn't sound like a lot of fun.

It's safe to say that *everyone* has some fears when it comes to traveling. But if you prepare and do your homework you can come home with plenty of fond memories, a few good rolls of film, and some great cocktail party chitchat material.

Making the initial call may seem like a daunting task, but most of the places you're getting in touch with have to be called for reservations anyway. Ensuring that your needs are evident from the start will help things flow more smoothly. The following steps will help you once you decide upon a vacation destination:

- Contact your destination's local Celiac Association (you'll find the list on page 171).
- Ask them where you can buy "free" treats, bread, pasta, etc. In much of Europe, these are found in a pharmacy, not a health food store.
- See if they have any restaurant or hotel suggestions and any other general advice that might help you. In Italy, for example, the national celiac association provides a list of approved restaurants that have a separate cooking facility for preparing gluten-free food. They are inspected regularly and must adhere to strict guidelines to maintain their status.
- Find out more about the culture's diet and what, typically, is "free" before you go.
- Call the airline to book a special meal for all flights (including connections).
- Call the hotel if you plan to have meals there, and advise the customer service manager or owner of your needs.
- Use a travel agent who's willing to address your needs with the various parties you may encounter, as well as help to get you the best arrangements possible (agents bring hotels and tour groups their business).
- Only book package tours with companies that are willing to take care of you. You need tour guides who are ready to speak to kitchen staff if you're going to be paying a package price that includes meals. If you're booking a cruise, make sure that the crew will be able to provide you with safe meals and will have "free" foods on board for you.
- It only takes a minute to write a gracious and informative letter that you can "CC" to all the parties involved in feeding you. This is extremely helpful for them, and is another form of insurance for you.
- Learn some emergency terms in the language. Do you know anyone who has traveled here before? Do you know anyone who hails from this place and speaks the language?
- If you're staying in one place and plan to stay close to the hotel, you can also bring your own bread, cookies, and muffins. Some people pack a box of staple foods and ship it to their hotel before they depart.
- Get a letter from your doctor if you're planning on traveling with food (some countries won't let you bring food across the border).

Yippee! The plane has landed and you're on your dream vacation. The sit-down meals are going to be a breeze, because you already know how to go about dining in restaurants. But what if you don't want your trip to revolve around three squares a day? Perhaps you're on a budget, or perhaps you'd rather spend more time trekking through cathedrals or vineyards than scoping out the locals in the bistros. It's important that you don't assume it'll be easy to find something safe to eat at any hour of the day. But little sandwich baggies of nuts, dried fruit, crackers, or cookies can be made up daily from your stash at the hotel. They're lightweight and will hold you over for a long time. And why not check out the local food markets? If you've packed your utensils and can opener, you'll have a lot more options.

Since breakfast is usually one of the more difficult things to grab on the run, opt for fruit. Bananas are particularly good because they fill you up. I like to save the calories for lunch, but you can also look for single serving yogurt or applesauce and cheese. Worse case scenario—buy a bottle of juice and build up an appetite.

For lunches on park benches, sitting around fountains or impromptu picnics, try:

- Cucumbers, baby carrots, radishes, fresh peas
- Cheese and simple smoked or cured meats
- Cans of tuna and salmon
- Grapes, apples, plums, peaches, cherries...
- Potato chips
- Rice cakes (you can find these almost anywhere now)
- Packages of peanuts, almonds, sesame seeds
- "Free" cookies and snacks (do you know where to find them yet?)
- Bottles of fruit juice or mineral water
- A bottle of wine (you can always enjoy it in your room if not on the street!)

Just remember: the simpler and more natural the food is, the less likely it will pose a problem. And once you get more comfortable with survival on foreign turf, you can take advantage of the opportunity to expand your culinary knowledge. Discover new foods. Make friends with the locals, and find out what interesting foods are native to them. Make a point of finding a shop or restaurant where you can try those foods. This is an adventure—and better than shopping for souvenirs.

Everyone travels differently. Some stay in posh hotels; others use a backpack. As you get into the swing of things, it'll all seem like less of a big deal. Finally, remember that if I can survive an entire year in Italy (the land of pizza and pasta), you can find food anywhere. Remember also that the only limitations are the ones that you impose on yourself. So get out there and taste life!

By Any Other Name

Flour has a lot of different names, and if you travel to another country, you need to know all of them. Find out how to say it, spell it, and—if you're going somewhere with a different alphabet—get someone to write down the symbols for you.

Learning just a little of a language can sometimes be just as dangerous as not knowing any, as sometimes the native speaker you're conversing with will assume you've made a mistake—and draw his or her own conclusions. Carry a language card with you when you travel. And ask the local Celiac Association to fax or email something to you. Keep more than one copy on you, in your camera case, pocket, purse, or wallet. This card is also handy when shopping. Where possible, ask the shopkeeper to help you verify what it is you're reading. When in doubt, rule it out.

Here are the words for gluten in four languages:

French

Wheat flour: *farine de blé, farine de froment, farine brute*
Rye: *seigle*
Barley: *orge*
Oats: *avoine, gruau*
Malt: *malt*
Gluten: *gluten*

I can't eat wheat flour or gluten:
Je ne peux pas manger de farine de ble ni de gluten.
Sounds like:
[Je ne pe pa manjay de fareen de blay nee de glooten.]

Spanish

Wheat flour: *harina de trigo*
Rye: *centeno*
Oats: *avena*
Barley: *cebada*
Malt: *malta*
Gluten: *gluten*

I can't eat wheat flour or gluten:
No puedo comer harina de trigo o gluten.
Sounds like:
[No pwedo comerrr arena day treego oh gluten.]

German

Wheat flour: *weizenhehl*
Rye: *roggen*
Oats: *hafer*
Barley: *gerste*
Malt: *malz*
Gluten: *gluten* (or) *kleber*

I can't eat wheat flour or gluten:
Ich kann veder weizenmehl noch gluten essen.
Sounds sort of like:
[Icghh kun vader viezenmail nocghh gluten essen.]

Italian

Wheat flour: *farina di grano*
Rye: *segala*
Oats: *avena*
Barley: *orzo*
Malt: *malto*
Gluten: *glutine*

I can't eat wheat flour or gluten:
Non posso mangiare farina di grano o glutine.
Sounds like:
[Non posso manjeearay fareena dee grano o glooteenay.]

Chapter 4 lists a website that allows you to download language cards to bring along when traveling. Looks like you're going to have an expanded vocabulary to show off to your travel companions!

Definitely Not the Epilogue

Finally, don't eat gluten. Don't buy gluten, order it in a restaurant, eat it at a friend's house, or on another continent. Don't be tempted by commercials, people who bake wheat bran muffins "just for you," or foods that have "just a little" gluten. Remember that most of the toxic stuff you're tempted to eat isn't healthy for anyone. Remember, too, that millions of people eat wheat- and gluten-free every day.

When you look beyond the restrictions of the typical North American diet, you can begin to feel empowered by your new-found food sense, and openness to new ideas. And your example just might inspire others to lead healthier and more fulfilling lives. Share your enthusiasm—and this book!

CELIAC ASSOCIATIONS WORLDWIDE

I contacted about 25 different celiac support groups around the world via email, and asked them whether or not they were able to assist people who wanted to travel to their country. I didn't hear back from everyone I contacted, but I was surprised to find just how helpful the people who responded were. Some mailed me the information I requested within the month; others emailed back, or directed me to specific websites. Some organizations also sent me language cards and lists of food manufacturers operating in their major cities. It was pretty neat! Anyway, it only takes a second to send a message, and you may just luck out.

What follows is a list of Celiac Associations and support groups, compiled April 2005. The majority were contacted and updated, but addresses—as we all know—do change. Your best bet is to try the websites and/or email addresses first. If you find yourself at a dead end, contact a neighboring Association, as they'll likely be able to provide you with the information you need.

Argentina *www.celiaco.org.ar*

Asistencia al Celiaco de la Argentina
Casilla de Correo 5555, Correo Central
1000 Buenos Aires
Republica Argentina
Tel: +54 114 2926373
Contact: Alicia Greco
Email: *acela@jede.net* or *correo@acela.org.ar*

Asociacion Celiaca Argentina – sede central
Calle 15 Nro.74, entre 33 y 34, (B1902CUD) – La Plata
Buenos Aires
Republica Argentina
Tel: +54 221 4838371
Fax: +54 221 4230927
Contact: Monica Pelusso
Email: *info@celiaco.org.ar*

Australia   *www.coeliac.org.au*

The Coeliac Society of NSW Inc.
PO Box 703, Chatwood
NSW 2057
Australia
Tel: +61 2 9411 4100
Fax: +61 2 9413 1296
Contact: Cheryl Price
Email: *info@nswcoeliac.org.au*
Website: *www.nswcoeliac.org.au*

Coeliac Society of South Australia Inc.
Unit 5/88 Glynburn Road, Hectorville
S.A. 5073
Australia
Tel: +61 8365 1488
Fax: +61 8365 1265
Website: *www.coeliac.org.au*

Coeliac Society of Western Australia
PO Box 1344
East Victoria Park
6981
Tel: +61 8 9470 4122
Fax: +61 8 9470 4166
Contact: Michelle Sladden

The Coeliac Society of Tasmania Inc.
PO Box 159, Launceston, 7250
Tasmania
Tel: +61 3 6427 2844
Fax: +61 3 6344 4284
Contact: Jo Quigley
Email: *coeliac_tas@vision.net.au*

The Queensland Coeliac Society Inc.
PO Box 2110 Fortitude Valley, BC
Queensland, 4006
Australia
Tel: +61 7 3393 1080
Fax: +61 7 3393 1787
Contact: Carol Nicolosi
Email: *coelqld@xenon.net*
Website: *www.qld.coeliac.org.au*

Coeliac Society of Victoria Inc.
PO Box 89, Holmesglen,
Victoria, 3148
Australia
Tel: +61 3 9808 5566
Fax: +61 3 9808 9922
Contact: Di Baker

Austria   *www.go.to.zoeliakie*

Oest. Arbeitsgemeinschaft Zöliakie
Anton-Baumgartner-Strasse, 44/C5/2302
A-1230 Wien
Austria
Tel: +43 1 667 1887
Fax: +43 1 667 1887 4
Contact: Hertha Deutsch
Email: *zoeliakie.oesterreich@utanet.at*

Belgium   *www.coeliakie.be*

S.M.B.C. – B.C.V.
International Contacts, Avenue Louis Bertrand 100
BTE A20 – 1030 Brussels
Belgium
Tel: +32 2 216 83 47
Fax: +32 2 216 8347
Contact: F. Vander Linden

Societe Belge De La Coeliaquie SBC.BCV
Rue Foulia G
WANZE, 4520
Belgium
Tel: +32 8 584 3159
Contact: Edith Weusten Radd

Vlaamse Coeliakie Vereniging
Den Bremt 36
B-3020 HERENT
Belgium
Tel: 32 1 623 8964
Email: celiac.flanders@skynet.be
Website: *www.vcv.coeliakie.be*

Bermuda

The Coeliac Support Group of Bermuda
PO Box 1556, Hamilton HM FX
Bermuda
Tel: +1 441 232 0264
Fax: +1 441 236 8387
Contact: Elizabeth Boden

Brazil

ACELBRA
Avenida Taquara, 586 sala 603, 90460-210 Porto Alegre
Rio Grande Do Sul
Brazil
Tel: +55 51 333 3000
Fax: +55 51 333 3000
Contact: Dr. Maria Luisa Guedes
Email: *acjpires@via-rs.net*

Bulgaria

Bulgarian Coeliac Society
Pl Slavieikov 9, Sofia 1000
Bulgaria
Contact: Isadora Zaidner

Canada   *www.celiac.ca*

Canadian Celiac Association
5170 Dixie Road, Suite 204
Mississauga, Ontario
L4W 1E3
Canada
Tel: +1 905 507 6208/1 800 363 7296
Fax: +1 905 507 4673
Email: *info@celiac.ca*

French Canada   *www.fqmc.org*

Fondation Québécoise de la Maladie Coeliaque
4837 rue Boyer, Bureau 230
Montreal, Quebec
H3W 2Z9
Canada
Tel: +1 514 529 8806
Fax: +1 514 529 2046
Email: *info@fqmc.org*

Chile

COACEL
Av.11 de Septembre 1945, OF 1118
Providencia Santiago
Chile
Tel: +56 2442828

Club de de Celiacos de la Universidad
Concepción, Urrutia Manzano 330
Concepción
Chile
Contact: Dr. Guillermo Bénegas

Croatia   *www.celiac.inet.hr*

Hrvatsko Drustvo za Celijakiju
41 000 Zagreb, Klaiczua 16
Klinika za Djecje Bolesti
Croatia
Tel: +385 1664514
Email: *celiac@inet.hr*

Cuba

Coeliac Society
Garrido 20708, Reparto Carolina
San Miguel del Padron, Habana
Cuba
Tel: +53 7914128
Contact: Edith Gonzalez

Czech Republic   *www.coeliac.cz*

Czech Coeliac Society
U Slovanky 7, 182 00 PRAHA 8
Czech Republic
Tel: +420 2 859 0654 (evenings/weekends)
Contact: Hana Maslowska
Email: *world@coeliac.cz*

Denmark   *www.coeliaki.dk*

Danish Celiac Society
Wilkensvej 16A, 4.th, DK-2000 Frederiksberg
Denmark
Tel: +45 7010 1003
Fax: +45 7010 1003
Contact: Christine Folkenæs
Email: *post@coeliaki.dk*

Estonia

Estonian Coeliac Society
Salu 11
79514 Rapla
Estonia
Tel: +372 48 96 824
Contact: Prof. Vello Salupere

Faroe Islands

Cöeliaki Felag Föroya
FR-510 Nordragöta
Faroe Islands
Tel: +298 4 1671
Fax: +298 4 1633
Contact: Marita Olsen
Email: *coliaki@post.olivant.fo*

Finland   *www.keliakia.org*

The Finnish Coeliac Society
Hammareninkatu 7, SF-33100 Tampere
Finland
Tel: +358 3 2541 321
Fax: +358 3 2541 350
Contact: Susanna Lohiniemi
Email: *info@keliakia.org*

France   *www.afdiag.com*

A.F.D.I.A.G.
15 Rue d'Hauteville
75010 Paris
Tel: +33 1 5608 0822
Fax: +33 1 5608 0842
Contact: Catherine Remillieux-Rast
Email: *afdiag.gluten@wanadoo.fr*

Germany   *www.dzg-online.de*

Deutsche Zöliakie-Gesellschaft e.V.
Filderhauptstrasse 61, D-70599 Stuttgart
Germany
Tel: +49 711 45 99 81 0
Fax: +49 711 45 99 81 50
Contact: Sofia Beisel
Email: *info@dzg-online.de*

Hungary

Lisztérzekenyek Erdekképviseletének
Országos Egyesülete, Palánta U.11
H-1025 Budapest
Hungary
Tel: +36 1 326 0770
Fax: +36 1 326 0770
Contact: Tunde Koltai
Email: *coeliac@c3.hu* or *coeliac@matavnet.hu*

Iceland

Samtok Folks med Glutenopol
Fannafold 231, IS-112 Reykjavik
Iceland
Tel: +354 860 3328
Fax: +354 560 3350
Contact: Magnus Asgeirsson
Email: *magnus@esso.is*

Ireland   *www.coeliac.ie*

The Coeliac Society of Ireland
Carmichael House, 4 North Brunswick Street
Dublin 7
Ireland
Tel: +353 1 872 1471
Fax: +353 1 873 5737
Contact: Ann Boland
Email: *coeliac@iol.ie*

Israel   *www.celiac.org.il*

The Celiac Association of Israel
40 Habiluyim Street
Ramat Gan 52297
Israel
Tel: +972 3 678 1481
Email: *office@celiac.org.il*

Italy   *www.celiachia.it*

A.I.C. – Associazione Italiana Celiachia
via Picotti 22, I-56124 Pisa
Italy
Tel: +39 50 580939
Fax: +39 50 580939
Contact: Anna Marie Vallesi
Email: *segretaria@celiachia.it*

Latvia

PO Box 1323
Riga, 1050
Latvia
Tel: +371 706 9636
Fax: +371 706 9661
Email: *Ieva1@caramail.com*

Lithuania

Lithuanian Coeliac Society
Vilius Univ. Children's Hospital
Center for Pediatrics
Santoriskiy-7 LTU-2600, Vilnius
Lithuania
Tel: +370 2720270
Fax: +370 2720368
Contact: Dr. Vaidotas Urbonas
Email: *uvaidas@cheerful.com*

Luxembourg   *www.alig.lu*

A.L.M.C.
4a, rue de la Paix, Dudelange
3541
Luxembourg
Tel: +352 52 02 79
Fax: +352 26 51 01 18
Contact: Francine Stocklausen
Email: *alig@pt.lu*

Malta

Coeliac Association Malta
Lamut, Upper Gardens
St Julians STJ 05
Malta
Tel: +356 21 370778
Contact: Mary Rose Caruana
Email: *edros@global.net.mt*

Netherlands   *www.coeliakievereniging.nl*

Nederlandse Coeliakie Vereniging
Postbus 65, NL 3860 AB Nijkerk
The Netherlands
Tel: +31 33 247 10 40
Fax: +31 33 247 10 42
Contact: Gerard Beerling
Email: *info@coeliakievereniging.nl*

New Zealand   *www.coeliac.co.nz*

Coeliac Society of New Zealand Inc.
PO Box 35 724
Browns Bay 1311, Dunedin
New Zealand
Tel: +64 09 820 5157
Fax: +64 09 820 5187
Contact: Kaye Ellis
Email: *coeliac@xtra.co.nz*

Norway   *www.ncf.no*

Norsk Coliakiforening
PO Box 4725
Nydalen 0421, Oslo
Norway
Tel: +47 22 79 91 70
Fax: +47 22 79 93 95
Email: *post@nfc.no*

Paraguay

FUPACEL, Fundación Paraguaya de Celíacos
Calle del Maestro, 32-38, Asunción
Paraguay
Tel: +595 2161 1880
Fax: +595 2161 1880
Contact: Elena Chamorro de Agullera

Poland

The Polish Coeliac Society
ul. Mantueffla 3/43, PL-03-988 Warszawa
Poland
Tel: +48 22 672 1835
Fax: +48 22 631 9921
Contact: Tomsz Kepka
Email: *gluten0@polbox.com*

Portugal

Clube dos Celiacos
Apartado 41005, 1500 Lisbon
Portugal
Tel: +351 96 323 0165
Contact: Dr. Paulo Ramalho
Email: *celiacos@iol.pt*

Clube dos Celiacos
Dept of Pediatrics, Hospital Sn Joao
4200 Porto
Portugal
Tel: +351 931 612 634
Fax: +351 2 525 766
Contact: Dr. Jorge Amil Dias

Romania

Aglutena Romania
sdr Avram Ianca no 24, RO – 2400 Sibiu
Romania
Tel: +40 69 21 76 22
Fax: +40 69 21 76 22
Contact: Karin Köber
Email: *Karin_koeber@web.de*

Russia

Naralina Kruschinskaja
UL. Ustriskova 8 Kv. 104, Moscow 125057
Russia
Fax: +7 095 242 9110

Slovenia   *www.drustvo-celiakija.si*

Slovensko Drustvo za Celiakijo
Ljubljanska 5, 2000 Maribor
Slovenia
Tel: +386 62 300 63 50
Fax: +386 62 300 63 50
Contact: Breda Kojc
Email: *drustvo@drustvo-celiakija.si*

South Africa

Coeliac Society of South Africa
Box No 64203, Highlands North 2037
Johannesburg
South Africa
Tel: +27 11 440 3431
Contact: M. Kaplan
Email: *coeliac@netactive.co.za*

Spain   *www.celiacos.org*

F.A.C.E.
C/Hileras, 45
28013, Madrid
Spain
Tel: +34 91 547 54 11
Fax: +34 91 541 06 64
Contact: Carlos Bravo
Email: *FACE.CBRAVO@terra.es*

S.M.A.P. Celiacs de Catalunya
Comtal, 32, 5e – 1a 08002
Barcelona
Spain
Tel: +34 93 412 17 89
Fax: +34 93 412 03 82
Email: *info@celiacscatalunya.org*
Website: *www.celiacscatalunya.org*

Sweden   *www.celiaki.se*

Svenska Celiakiförbundet (SCF)
Box 1160, S-17123 Solna
Sweden
Tel: +46 8 730 05 01
Fax: +46 8 730 05 02
Contact: Björn Johansson
Email: *kansli@celiaki.se*

Switzerland   *www.coeliakie.ch*

Association Romande de la Coeliakie
Route du Lac 2, CH 1094 Paudex
Case postale 1215 CH 1001
Lausanne
Switzerland
Tel: +41 21 796 3300
Fax: +41 21 796 3311
Contact: Jean-Francois Tosetti
Email: *info@coeliakie.ch*

Gruppo Celiachia
della Swizzera Italiana
Casella postale 113
CH-6592 S. Antonio
Switzerland
Tel: +41 79 714 07 79
Fax: +41 91 858 36 08
Contact: Mimi Tamagni
Email: *100578@tichino.com*

Schweizerische Interessengemeinschaft
für Zöliakie,
Birmannsgasse 20
4055 Basel
Switzerland
Tel: +41 61 271 62 17
Fax: +41 61 271 62 18
Contact: Anita Dimas
Website: *www.zoeliakie.ch*
Email: *dimas@rol3.com* or *sekretariat@zoeliakie.ch*

United Kingdom *www.coeliac.co.uk*

The Coeliac Society
PO Box No 220, High Wycombe
Bucks HP11 2HY
United Kingdom
Tel: +44 1494 437278
Fax: +44 1494 474349
Contact: Jean Austin
Email: *admin@coeliac.co.uk*

United States

CSA/USA Inc.
PO Box 31700
Omaha, NE 68131-0700
USA
Tel: +1 402 558 0600
Fax: +1 402 558 1347
Website: *www.csaceliacs.org*
Email: *celiacs@csaceliacs.org*

Celiac Disease Foundation
13251 Ventura Boulevard, Suite 1
Studio City, CA 91604-1838
USA
Tel: +1 818 990 2354
Fax: +1 818 990 2379
Contact: Elaine Monarch
Website: *www.celiac.org*
Email: *cdf@primenet.com* or *cdf@celiac.org*

Gluten Intolernace Group, North America
15110-10th Ave SW, Suite A
Seattle, WA 98166-1820
USA
Tel: +1 206 246 6652
Fax: +1 206 246 6531
Contact: Cynthia Kupper
Website: *www.gluten.net*
Email: *gig@accessone.com* or *gig@gluten.net*

The American Celiac Society
58 Musano Ct
West Orange, NJ 07052
USA
Tel: +1 973 325 8837
Fax: +1 973 669 8808
Contact: Annette Bentley
Email: *amerceliacsoc@netscape.net*

Uruguay   *www.acelu.org*

Asociation Celiaca del Uruguay (ACELU)
Canelones 1164, Montevideo
Uruguay
Tel: +598 2 902 2362 63
Fax: +598 2 908 5959
Contact: Haydee Fachelli de Claramunt
Email: *fclara@st.com.uy*

BIBLIOGRAPHY

Barker, Collin C., M.D., and J. Decker Butzner, M.D., F.R.C.P.(C.). "Screening for Celiac Disease, An Idea Whose Time Has Come." (2001 15: 1: 13) *Celiac News*, Publication of the Canadian Celiac Association.

Campbell, Alex J., Ph.D., and Zarkadas, M.Sc. *Acceptability of Foods and Food Ingredients for the Gluten-Free Diet. Pocket Dictionary.* (Mississauga, Ontario: The Canadian Celiac Association, 1992.)

Campbell, Alex J., Ph.D. "The Question of Gluten in Distilled Alcohol." (1998 12: 3: 10) *Celiac News*, Publication of the Canadian Celiac Association.

The Canadian Celiac Association Handbook: Celiac Disease needs a diet for life, 3rd ed. (Mississauga, Ontario: The Canadian Celiac Association, 1993.)

Clemente, MG, S. De Virgiliis, JS Kang, R. Macatagney, MP Musu, MR Di Pierro, S. Drago, M. Congia, and A. Fasano. "Early effects of gliadin on enterocyte intracellular signalling involved in intestinal barrier function." (2003: 52(2): 218–23) *Gut*.

The Coeliac Handbook, 3rd ed. (London, England: The Coeliac Society, 1972.)

Eliakim, R. "Wireless capsule video endoscopy: three years of experience." (2004: 1: 10(9): 1238–9) *World J Gastroenterology*.

Enns, R., K. Go, K. Chang, and K. Pluta. "Capsule endoscopy: a single-centre experience with the first 226 capsules." (2004: 18(9): 555–8) *Can J Gastroenterol*.

Fasano, Alessio, M.D. "Celiac Disease: the Past, the Present, the Future." (Notes from address to Canadian National Celiac Conference, Winnipeg, Manitoba: May 2001.)

Fasano, A., T. Not, W. Wang, S. Uzzau, I. Berti, A. Tommasini, and SE Goldblum. "Zonulin, a newly discovered modulator of intestinal permeability, and its expression in celiac disease." (2000: 29: 355(9214): 1518–9) *Lancet.*

Gardner, Joy. *The New Healing Yourself: Natural Remedies for Adults and Children,* 7th ed. (Freedom, California: The Crossing Press, 1989.)

Gottschall, Elaine, B.A., M.Sc. *Food and the Gut Reaction: Intestinal Health Through Diet,* 6th ed. (Kirkton, Ontario: Kirkton Press, 1992.)

Greenberg, Ronald, M.D. and Angela Nori. *Freedom from Allergy Cookbook,* 2nd ed. (Vancouver, British Columbia: Blue Poppy Press, 1996.)

Hagman, Bette. *The Gluten-Free Gourmet: Living Well Without Wheat.* (New York: Henry Holt and Company, Inc., 1990.)

Hagman, Bette. *The Gluten-Free Gourmet Cooks Fast and Healthy.* (New York: Henry Holt and Company, Inc., 1996.)

Hills, Hilda Cherry. *Good Food, Gluten Free.* (New Canaan, Connecticut: Keats Publishing Inc., 1976.)

Hunter, John, M.D., Virginia Alun Jones, M.D., and Elizabeth Workman, R.D. *Food Intolerance.* (Tuscon, Arizona: The Body Press, 1986.)

"Information Guide to the Labeling of Alcoholic Beverages."
Agriculture and Agri-Food Canada, Food Division, January 1996.

Issenman, Robert, M.D. "Address." Canadian National Celiac Conference. Hamilton, Ontario: May 2000.

Maki, Markku, M.D. "Address." Canadian National Celiac Conference. Hamilton, Ontario: May 2000.

Marti, T. O. Molberg, Q. Li, GM Gray, C. Khosla, and LM Sollid. "Prolyl endopeptidase-mediated destruction of T cell epitopes in whole gluten: chemical and immunological characterization." Celiac Sprue Research Foundation. (2005: 312(1): 19–26. Epub 2004 Sep 9) *J Pharmacol Exp Ther.*

Rawcliffe, Peter, M.D. and Ruth Rolph, S.R.D. *The Gluten-Free Diet Book.* (Toronto, Ontario: New Canadian Publications, 1985.)

Rottmann, Leon H. *On the Celiac Condition: A Handbook for Celiac Patients and Their Families*, 2nd ed. (Omaha, Nebraska: Celiac Sprue Association, United States of America, Inc., 1998.)

Smecuol, E., E. Sugai, S. Niveloni, H. Vazquez, S. Pedreira, R. Mazure, ML Moreno, M. Label, E. Maurino, A. Fasano, J. Meddings, and JC Bai. "Permeability, zonulin production, and enteropathy in dermatitis herpetiformis." (2005: 3(4): 335–41) *Clin Gastroenterol Hepatol.*

St. John's University, listserv. *listserv@maelstrom.stjohns.edu.*

Wight, Quintin. "Hydrolyzed Vegetable Protein." (1999 13:2) *Celiac News*, Publication of the Canadian Celiac Association.

Wodzinska, JM. "Transglutaminases as targets for pharmacological inhibition." (2005: 5(3): 279–92) *Mini Rev Med Chem.*

Wood, Rebecca. *The Splendid Grain.* (New York: William Morrow and Co. Inc., 1997.)

GLOSSARY OF TERMS

Acidophilus: "Friendly" bacteria found in the digestive tract. Occurs naturally in yogurt, and can also be consumed in pill form.

Amaranth: Small, starchy seeds from the amaranth plant that are very high in protein and are usually milled into flour.

Antibody: A special protein that is part of your body's immune system. White blood cells make antibodies to neutralize harmful germs or other foreign substances, called antigens.

Autoimmune diseases: The immune system makes antibodies to protect itself by destroying antigens. Autoimmune diseases are caused by a failure of the body to distinguish between foreign antigens and self.

Baking powder: A mixture of sodium bicarbonate, cream of tartar, and, often, wheat starch.

Barley: A hardy cereal containing gluten.

Biopsy: An examination of tissue that has been removed from a living body to discover the presence, cause, or extent of a disease.

Buckwheat: A grass, not a grain as the name implies, that is not related to wheat.

Bulgar: A cereal food of whole wheat partially boiled then dried and cracked. Contains gluten.

Candida: Any yeastlike parasitic fungus (e.g., thrush).

Couscous: A North African dish of coarsely ground wheat steamed with broth. Contains gluten.

Crohn's disease: A disease affecting any part of the digestive tract, but most commonly lesions in the ileum and colon. Patients suffer from digestive complaints as well as a lack of energy.

Dextrin: A soluble, gummy substance obtained from the starch of corn, potato, tapioca, rice, or wheat.

Duodenum: The first part of the small intestine, immediately below the stomach.

Distilled alcohol: Created through the purification of a liquid by vaporizing it with heat, then condensing it with cold and collecting the result. Distilled alcohol is made from a mash of cereal grains or sugar.

Durum wheat: A kind of wheat that has hard seeds and yields a flour used in the manufacturing of pasta. Contains gluten.

Endoscope: An instrument for viewing internal parts of the body.

Farina: The flour or meal of cereal, nuts, or starchy foods. In Britain, it can be used as "starch." May contain gluten.

Fibromyalgia: A specific, chronic systemic pain condition. Tender points occur in pairs on various parts of the body.

Flour: Flour as an ingredient means wheat flour, white flour, enriched flour, or enriched white flour, all of which contain gluten.

Gene: A unit of heredity composed of DNA or RNA, which forms the part of a chromosome that determines a particular characteristic of an individual.

Genetic disorder: A disorder that occurs as a result of one's genetic make-up (see above).

Gliadin: A class of protein found in gluten. Gliadin is the fraction of gluten that the body reacts to when a person has celiac disease.

192

Gluten: A sticky protein that gives structure to baked products. Found in wheat, rye, oats, triticale, and barley.

Gluten flour: Wheat flour that has had some of the starch removed to increase the ratio of gluten.

Graham flour: Wheat flour to which other parts of the wheat plant have been added. Contains gluten.

HPP: Hydrolyzed plant protein, used to enhance flavor. HPP is produced via the chemical reaction of water with another substance, such as soy, rice, or wheat.

HVP: Hydrolyzed vegetable protein (see above).

IgA-antiendomysium (EmA) and IgA-tissue transglutaminase (tTG): Blood tests that detect the presence of specific antibodies. These are two of the newer blood tests used for screening and are both used in combination for diagnosis purposes.

Irritable bowel syndrome: Characterized by a severely sensitive or aggravated digestive system with chronic bouts of diarrhea often followed by constipation. Believed to be triggered by stress.

Jejunum: The part of the small intestine between the duodenum and the ileum.

Kamut: A type of durum wheat. Contains gluten.

Lymphoma: Cancer of the lymphatic system.

Malt: Barley or other grain that is steeped, germinated, and dried. Contains gluten.

Malt extract/malt flavoring: An extract of malt, used as a flavoring agent. Contains gluten.

Malt syrup: Syrup derived from malt, used as a flavoring agent. Contains gluten.

Millet: A plant closely related to corn. Bears small, nutritious seeds.

Modified starch: Starch that has been modified by a chemical treatment to alter its characteristics. Starch may be from many sources, such as rice, corn, soy, or wheat.

Monosodium glutamate (MSG): A sodium salt of glutamic acid used to flavor food.

Oats: A cereal grain. Gluten-containing status still in question.

Osteoporosis: A condition characterized by brittle and fragile bones caused by loss of bony tissue as a result of hormonal changes, or a deficiency of calcium and vitamin D.

Protein: Any group of organic compounds composed of one or more chains of amino acids. An essential part of all living organisms.

Quinoa: Light textured seeds from the pigweed family.

Rye: A cereal grain containing gluten.

Semolina: The hard grains left after the milling of flour, used in puddings and pasta. Contains gluten.

Small intestine: The intestine is the canal from the end of the stomach to the anus. The small intestine is the beginning section of this canal, and is made up of the duodenum, jejunum, and ileum collectively.

Soy sauce: A sauce made in China and Japan from pickled soya beans. Can be thickened with wheat flour.

Spelt: A species of wheat, also called dinkel or German wheat. Contains gluten.

Triticale: A cereal that is a cross between wheat and rye. Contains gluten.

Villi: The short, finger-like projections on the mucus membrane of the small intestine

Wheat bran: The husk of the wheat, used as a source of fiber in the diet. Contains gluten.

Wheat germ: The embryo of the wheat grain, extracted as a source of vitamins. Contains gluten.

Wheat starch: The result of removing *most* of the gluten from wheat flour. Contains gluten.

INDEX

ISBN 155369404-X

9 781553 694045

Made in the USA